Not Normal

Not Normal

A Progressive's Diary of the Year After Trump's Election

Stuart Shapiro

ISBN-13: 9781979634670
ISBN-10: 197963467X

Acknowledgements

When I started writing this diary, I had no idea it would go on as long as it did. The entries continued because of the encouraging feedback and comments I received from friends. And the entries themselves were inspired by conversations with many of these individuals. In particular I need to thank Anne Gowen, Daniel Finaldi, and Chris Virden for many such conversations. I also need to thank Jean Kwok and Paula Kluth for encouraging me to expand my audience and move forward with this book.

Prologue: November 8, 2016

As I had in 2012, I agreed to host the graduate students at my school, the Bloustein School of Planning and Public Policy, for a pizza party at the school on election night. I would provide insights as the returns came in both for the presidential election and control of the Senate. It was going to be fun. I got to play pundit (usually I am more policy wonk than political pundit), and all indications were that the students were going to be happy with the election results.

I did have some nagging concerns, of course. That morning, Nate Silver, whom I largely swear by, gave Trump a 30 percent chance of winning the election. Most people reacted to this in one of two ways:

- Hillary's gonna win!
- Silver just has a higher number because he likes to get clicks on his website.

I had neither of these reactions. To me it meant that the chance of Trump winning was the same as a .300 hitter in baseball getting a hit in any given at bat. And we consider .300 hitters as good hitters. But they still make outs most of the time.

One other thing bothered me. While some were touting the Hispanic turnout in the early voting in North Carolina as a sign that Hillary might win Arizona, I had read some analysis of early voting in Upstate New York. Trump was doing surprisingly well. And I said to myself, "Upstate New York looks a lot like the Midwest demographically, working class and white."

Still I don't want to pretend I had more insights than others. I thought Hillary was going to win and perhaps would win convincingly. And as the night got started, the early results went as predicted. The mood in the room was jovial.

I don't remember exactly when it started to go south. Sometime between 8:30 p.m. and 9:00 p.m. I think when states that Hillary was supposed to win (especially Pennsylvania, Michigan, and Wisconsin, which no Democrat had lost since Michael Dukakis) were dubbed "too close to call." With Florida looking like it would go for Trump, Hillary could not afford to lose any of those states, much less all of them.

As some students and I studied which counties had not yet reported, by 10:00 p.m. it was clear that things were going very badly. I left the students at 11:00 p.m., telling them that Trump would be president unless a miracle occurred. I went home to my wife to watch the coverage until 2:30 a.m., hoping for that miracle. It didn't happen.

While I don't pretend to have predicted Trump's victory, I take full credit in thinking he would be a disaster as president. In the Republican primaries, I treated him as a joke at first. I bet a steak dinner with a friend that none of the outsiders (Trump, Carson, or Fiorina) would get the nomination. Once it became clear after New Hampshire that he was no joke, I rooted hard against him, even hoping the reprehensible Ted Cruz would beat him. Trump's combination of racial demagoguery, vanity, and lack of knowledge about government terrified me.

So I woke up on the rainy morning of November 9, 2016, nauseated at the thought of him as president. Since I could only complain to my wife so much, I took to Facebook to vent. I never really stopped venting. The result is reproduced below and contains my reactions to Trump as 2016 turned to 2017. The entries have been copyedited, but nothing of substance has been changed. Unlike this entry, the entries below are in real time, so they reflect my thinking at the time they were written. Sometimes my thinking changed as the year went on, and that will become apparent as you read through them. And yes, his presidency has been worse than even I imagined.

NOVEMBER 9, 2016—THE MORNING AFTER

Many people are unburdening themselves on Facebook this morning (thank you my wonderful friends for your moving comments). So here I go.

Events like this can and should force us to rethink what we believe in. For me, I believe most deeply in democracy. In America we don't let a bunch of people in a room make a decision about the future of the country. We've designed a system that for two hundred years has allowed the expression of the will of the people without allowing the agglomeration of power.

But this morning, all that is in question. The people chose a demagogue (I know he didn't win the popular vote, so if it makes it easier, substitute the words "fifty-seven million" for the word "the" in the previous sentence). Not the media, not the elites—the people. The other two branches are controlled by those who seem more inclined to facilitate him than to check him. This is not Bush; this is not Reagan. If this can happen, we need to (a) fight to ensure our democracy does not perish and that those who are most vulnerable do not spend the next four years in terror and (b) figure out what needs to change so it can never happen again.

Can our institutions survive? We are fond of bragging of the strength of our governmental structure (I have done it frequently myself). They will be tested in the next four years. To some degree we will be very dependent on people like Senators McCain and Graham and (yes) James Comey. At some point I suspect that they will be asked to acquiesce in actions that undermine the rule of law. Will they stand up? I don't know.

A few other random thoughts:

1. This election was first and foremost about race and gender. Yes, many of those who voted for Trump are anxious about their economic futures (largely for reasons outside the control of politicians frankly), but they have decided to blame that anxiety on those who do not look like them. As one of my Facebook friends put it, I am just as angry at those who held their nose and tolerated his fostering of racism as I am at those who gleefully did so.

2. Yes, the polls were wrong, but they weren't that wrong. Hillary won by a point when the final polls averaged out to her winning

by three points. That's an error, but it's not a huge one. Instead those like (my hero) Nate Silver, who pointed out last week that Trump had a very real chance at victory, were pilloried by those who wanted it to not be true.

3. I feel awful for Hillary Clinton this morning. She was far from a perfect candidate. But no one deserves going through what she went through over the past six months (and yes thirty years). Did she react badly to these pressures at times? Sure, but I don't know who among us would have been better. And now, she may have cause to be worried about her personal freedom and safety.

4. As many of you know, we were in the White House this past weekend. For me that just adds to my sadness today.

5. God bless you all.

NOVEMBER 16, 2016: MY ANALYSIS OF THE 2016 ELECTION (ORIGINALLY APPEARED IN THE *HILL*)[1]

After last week's presidential election, there has been much hand wringing about how Democrats can communicate with the Rust Belt voters who turned on them.

On the one hand, that is natural; the losses in Pennsylvania, Wisconsin, and Michigan were surprising and achingly close. And Democrats are well known for their propensity to wring their hands.

But it may also be exactly the wrong approach for a changing American electorate.

The Rust Belt states have been hard hit economically as manufacturing and coal-based jobs have left in droves. It's true that President Obama's policies (outside of rescuing the auto industry—a benefit for which he received credit in 2012 but one he did not transfer to Democratic nominee Hillary Clinton) did not do much to alter this trend.

---

1 Stuart Shapiro, "Democrats Should Probably Move on from the Rust Belt," *The Hill*, November 16, 2016. http://thehill.com/blogs/pundits-blog/campaign/306312-democrats-should-probably-just-move-on-from-the-rust-belt

It is also likely, absent a massive public-spending program on infrastructure, that President-elect Donald Trump will not be able to change this trend either.

Globalization and automation are not going away. And even Senate Majority Leader Mitch McConnell (R-Ky.) admits that reversing Obama's policies will not help the coal industry.

In other words, the Rust Belt is difficult terrain moving forward for both parties.

Democrats may be gleefully looking forward to blaming Trump for his failure to restore the Midwestern economy in 2020. But such an economy is likely to be even more fertile ground for the politics of resentment that Trump so thoroughly and effectively used this year.

A closer look at recent election data reveals another approach. Seventeen states were decided by 10 percentage points or fewer in the election last week. One could argue that these states are the most likely Electoral College battlegrounds in 2020.

Of these seventeen states, Clinton improved on Obama's 2012 percentages in four of them: Texas, Georgia, Arizona, and Virginia. The five states that she did not improve on Obama's performance but came closest were Florida, North Carolina, Colorado, Nevada, and New Mexico.

Let's call these nine states the Democratic Opportunity States. The other eight states were all in the Rust Belt or in New England.

The Democratic Opportunity States all have three important things in common.

Eight of them have higher nonwhite populations than the eight states that trended the furthest away from the Democrats (Michigan is slightly more diverse than Colorado).

The Democratic Opportunity States have also had greater population growth than the other states, meaning their share of the Electoral College will grow.

And finally, the Democratic Opportunity States are less reliant upon manufacturing than the others.

A Democratic Party that has its eyes on the future should focus on either winning or consolidating their gains in these nine states, particularly in presidential politics.

Of course, the Democrats should continue to run candidates for Senate, the House of Representatives, and state and local offices in the Rust Belt (and everywhere) that reflect the concerns of these states. To do otherwise would be foolish.

But as the Democrats look forward to 2020 and beyond, their resources (for voter registration and turnout in particular) should be devoted first and foremost to areas where the wind is at their backs and demographic and economic trends favor them.

To paraphrase Horace Greeley, they should go West (and South).

NOVEMBER 18, 2016: THE FIRST APPOINTMENTS

Three of Trump's first four appointees (Bannon, Flynn, and Sessions) can credibly be accused of racism. This should surprise no one (first rule of authoritarians—believe what they say).

NOVEMBER 21, 2016: MY RESPONSE TO CLAIMS THAT IT'S "NOT ABOUT RACE"

You northern and eastern elites really never took the trouble to understand our concerns. Your support of tariffs on manufactured goods and opposition to tariffs on raw materials were destroying our way of life. That's why we seceded. It has nothing to do with slavery.

DECEMBER 15, 2016: THE CIA REPORT COMES OUT (ORIGINALLY APPEARED IN THE *HILL*)[2]

Last week, it was revealed that the CIA had concluded that Russia was responsible for the hack of Democratic National Committee e-mails. Furthermore, they had done so in an attempt to influence the 2016 presidential election.

---

2 Stuart Shapiro, "Why You Can't Just Ignore the CIA Report on Russia," *The Hill* December 15, 2016, http://thehill.com/blogs/pundits-blog/homeland-security/ 310509-why-you-cant-just-ignore-the-cia-report-on-russia.

Supporters of Democratic nominee Hillary Clinton (like me, admittedly) jumped on this news and generally accepted its veracity. Supporters of President-elect Donald Trump (led by Trump himself) openly questioned the CIA's findings.

If the CIA had concluded that Clinton had promised favors to international potentates who donated to the Clinton Foundation, I suspect that reactions to the quality of the analysis would have been reversed.

But whether the CIA is good at its job is not a partisan issue. Or at least, it shouldn't be.

How we treat the conclusions of experts has become increasingly partisan, and the 2016 election has accelerated this trend at warp speed. The potential long-term damage of this trend is deeply consequential.

Experts are not entirely blameless, as too often they assert their conclusions with greater confidence than their underlying analysis merits. This is particularly true when experts are making predictions about the future rather than explaining what has happened in the past. When these experts use their platform to gain personal attention, they further diminish the credibility of experts everywhere.

But expertise does matter. When 97 percent of scientists agree that humans have contributed to climate change, that means something. Sure, scientific consensus can be wrong. Skeptics of consensus always love to claim that they are Galileo or Darwin, but it is important to remember that these examples represent a once-per-century phenomenon.

Social science or intelligence analysis will never produce conclusions that are as certain as science. But that uncertainty is not an excuse to dismiss the enterprise of expert analysis in nonscientific fields altogether.

If it were, we might as well choose our public policies at random. More than two hundred years of post-Enlightenment reasoning have taught us that instead of randomness, we should use the scientific method and critical thinking to make decisions. That is what experts give us.

Are experts biased? Sure. Do they make mistakes? Absolutely. Economists tend to see things through the lens of their training. So do lawyers, and so do intelligence experts at the CIA.

But an effectively functioning bureaucracy sets up its analytical process by asking a large number of people to weigh in on a decision and making sure they all get heard. This can lead to groupthink, but again, this is a reason to examine conclusions more carefully, not simply dismiss them as the president-elect did with the CIA conclusions.

If I'm being honest with myself, I don't know for sure if the CIA conclusion about Russian interference with the election is correct. But neither do you. And most alarmingly, as he skips out on his daily intelligence briefings, neither does the president-elect.

The fact that a group of experts that knows better than you, I, or Trump thinks that the "political equivalent of 9/11," as former CIA Director Michael Morell described it, could have happened means that we should examine the question in much more detail and have other independent experts conduct their own analysis.

Any other conclusion is the equivalent of saying "I don't care what experts say. I don't need those vegetables. I'll just eat Twinkies."

Good luck with that.

JANUARY 8, 2017: THE TRUMP ADMINISTRATION COMES INTO FOCUS

Influenced by a Paul Krugman tweetstorm the other day,[3] I've begun to wonder how this all ends. How does the surreal tragedy that was the 2016 campaign and the Trump presidency end? Obviously it is way too early to know, but I can foresee four scenarios. In decreasing order of likelihood in my mind, they are as follows:

1. Thanks to continual pressure from the media and people like us, an examination of Trump's connections to Russian interference in the US election and his conflicts of interest continues. Spearheaded by Republican senators like McCain and Graham,

---

3 Paul Krugman on twitter.com January 6, 2017, https://twitter.com/paulkrugman/status/817447039273467904.

investigations in the Senate are unrelenting, and eventually a smoking gun is found. Trump is faced with impeachment (we are faced with a constitutional crisis unlike any since Watergate) and ends up out of office. President Pence runs for reelection in 2020.

2. Not inconsistent with #1: Some stark event leads to a crisis. Putin invades Latvia, and Trump does nothing. Bannon is caught working with Russia trying to bring down Merkel in Germany. Trump announces that elections in 2018 will be delayed. We are faced with a constitutional crisis that makes Watergate look like child's play. The reaction is strong enough to force him out of office. President Pence runs for reelection in 2020.

3. Trump and Bannon quickly erode civil liberties. A terrorist attack occurs, and AG Sessions announces that newspapers that criticize Trump will be shut down. An example is made of the *Washington Post*. People are jailed for their tweets or Facebook posts. The chilling effect is quick, and even if the events in #2 occur, there are not enough people to speak out. There is no real election in 2020, and Trump Jr. eventually succeeds his father as president.

4. Trump mildly criticizes Russia and investigations back off. He ends up being a conservative president signing legislation that Ryan passes (gutting Medicaid and Food Stamps, repealing the ACA) and making public appearances to rally his supporters. He runs for reelection in 2020.

The difference between ending up in #3 and #1, #2, or #4 is us. We have to be ready to protest, call your congressperson repeatedly (particularly if you live in a red district or state), and yes share your outrage on Twitter and Facebook. If your issue is education or environment or health care, by all means fight on those fronts. But also be ready to fight to protect our democratic institutions like rule of law, freedom of the press, and civil liberties. You may have to support some people you disagree with on those other issues. It will be worth it. Everything matters now.

JANUARY 11, 2017: THE ONE HUNDREDTH ANNIVERSARY OF WORLD WAR I

A hundred years ago this year, we entered World War I: Here is a description of what followed. It shows how quickly things can go bad:

> No matter how familiar one is with the era, it is still shocking to read the breathtaking swiftness with which the country flipped into reaction once war was declared. A national vigilante group, the American Protective League, encouraged by the authorities, took to stopping men on the street to check for "slackers." The Espionage and Sedition Acts of 1917-18, passed by a suddenly belligerent Congress, were the most outrageously unconstitutional violations of our civil liberties since the 1798 Alien and Sedition Acts. The Supreme Court supinely upheld this legislation, and the Wilson administration ruthlessly exploited it, censoring the mails, shutting down publications and sentencing the likes of Eugene V. Debs, the gentle 63-year-old Socialist leader, to jail for 10 years for making a speech indirectly questioning the draft. The waves of reaction rolled on after the Armistice. Strikes were brutally crushed and labor unions all but annihilated. Black churches and neighborhoods were burned to the ground, and hundreds, maybe thousands of African-Americans murdered in white-on-black pogroms. Civil liberties continued to be curtailed, elected Socialist leaders were thrown out of office and radicals like Emma Goldman were deported.[4]

JANUARY 13, 2017: TRUMP'S CABINET

I called my senators today to urge them to oppose seven of Trump's nominees for cabinet positions. This is not something I expected to do. I start

---

4 Kevin Baker, "The War to Stay Out of the War Against War," *New York Times,* January 4, 2017, https://www.nytimes.com/2017/01/04/books/review/war-against-war-michael-kazin.html?_r=0.

with the presumption that the president should get to pick the people who work for him. The burden of proof is on those who oppose the choice (judges are at least somewhat different). John Ashcroft is the only nominee I can remember feeling this way about (and I worded for the feds then so I did not call). Having said that (here it comes), there are two reasons to oppose a president's cabinet choice.

1. The person is unqualified by dint of a lack of knowledge in the subject area or because of ethical or legal questions.
2. The views of the individual are so awful in your view that they will cause untoward damage to the area of policy they are being selected to oversee.

One other factor played into my ranking of the Trump nominees, all cabinet positions are not created equal. A horrible choice for secretary of agriculture (Trump has not yet nominated someone) is not the same as a horrible choice for secretary of state. With that in mind, there are three tiers of Trump nominees in my mind.

Tier 1: Aaaaaaaahhhhh!
Senator Jeff Sessions, justice. Employing a man with a history of racist actions to oversee enforcement of our civil rights and elections laws. Employing a man in favor of torture as a key figure in the War on Terror. Simply put, he makes Ashcroft look good.

Tier 1a: Some chance this guy could be OK but not sure we can take the chance.
Rex Tillerson, state. He believes in climate change (a low bar I know). He's divesting his holdings. He's said he will be tougher on Russia than Trump has indicated. But those Russia ties are alarming. Especially given his lack of experience. Our last five secretaries of state: Kerry, Clinton, Rice, Powell, and Albright. Think about that.

Tier 2: Bad nominees and in my mind worth fighting but it won't be the end of the Republic if they are confirmed.

In order of concern. Tom Price, HHS (scary views, very important department); Scott Pruitt, EPA (scary views, very important department); Andrew Puzder, Labor (scary views, arguably unqualified, important department); Betsy DeVos, Education (scary views, may be unqualified); Ben Carson, HUD (the least qualified nominee I can remember).

Tier 3: Fine, confirm them.

In order of concern. Rick Perry, Energy John Kelly, DHS; Ryan Zinke, Interior; Wilbur Ross, Commerce; David Shulkin, VA; James Mattis, Defense (actually hoping he is confirmed immediately). I would suspect that when Trump nominates someone for Agriculture, I would not oppose them (but he is clearly capable of surprising us).

JANUARY 14, 2017: A BUSY WEEKEND

In the past forty-eight hours:

Marine Le Pen French far-right-wing presidential candidate met in Trump Tower with a colleague of Steve Bannon.

Newt Gingrich said that Trump "can close down the elite press."

Republican Congressman Jason Chaffetz "requested a meeting" with the head of the Office of Government Ethics, Walter Shaub, a day after Shaub questioned Trump's plans regarding his conflicts of interests (and threatened a subpoena if Shaub didn't agree to the meeting).

Trump announced his first trip to meet with a foreign leader will be to see Justin Trudeau (no, just kidding it's gonna be Vladimir Putin).

And this doesn't even get to the intelligence stuff (still very murky) or the John Lewis kerfuffle (deeply offensive but a distraction again).

Tell me how this might end up OK.

JANUARY 21, 2017: THE WOMEN'S MARCH

In DC today with five hundred thousand of my closest friends. Other than perhaps the day Obama was elected, the proudest I've been of my country.

JANUARY 22, 2017: THE MCCONNELL-RYAN GAMBLE

Two things I saw today crystallized for me something I've been thinking about lately. The first is the Robert Reich post below.[5] The second is in the first comment about the Spicer press diatribe yesterday.

Ryan and McConnell are gambling that they can pass their desired legislation (tax cuts, program cuts, and Obamacare dismantling) before Trump implodes, and they have to impeach him and put Pence in (as Reich describes below).

Bannon and Trump are gambling that they can achieve their aims: Trump lining his pockets and Bannon establishing an authoritarian state before Ryan and McConnell wake up, and by then it will be too late. Then he can make Congress purely ceremonial.

It's our job to make sure they both lose their gambles, if either one wins, it is a calamity for our country (Trump-Bannon worse in my view but Ryan-McConnell awful too). Yesterday's march was a start, but there is a lot more work to do.

JANUARY 24, 2017: NORMAL VERSUS NOT NORMAL

As all the talk of normalizing Trump continues, I think it is important to distinguish between Trump's actions that are "normal" and "not normal." By "normal" I mean behaving like a typical Republican president. I don't mean I agree with the actions, and I don't mean that you shouldn't fight them. But since there are extraordinary things taking place, it's important to be aware of them and give them particular attention.

NORMAL: Freezing all the regulatory actions of his predecessor that were not yet complete. Bush and indeed Obama did the same thing.

NOT NORMAL: Having your press secretary harangue the press about reporting on crowd sizes, then having one of your top advisers defend the use of "alternative facts." Finally having your press secretary then lie several more times the next time he meets the press.

---

5 The Reich Facebook post can be found here: https://www.facebook.com/RBReich/posts/1445206565491935.

NORMAL: Reinstating the global gag rule on abortion. This is exactly what Reagan and Bush did.

NOT NORMAL: Going to the CIA, standing in front of a wall listing fallen CIA members, never mentioning the wall, and complaining about your media coverage. Also, bringing people to the CIA to clap for you as you do this.

NOT NORMAL: Continuing to assert that you would have won the popular vote if it weren't for three million illegal voters.

NORMAL: Getting full party support for your cabinet nominees.

NOT NORMAL: Having five nominees never having served in government before, and clearly demonstrating their lack of understanding at their confirmation hearings (Tillerson, Carson, DeVos, Ross [his confirmation hearings were actually OK], and Mnuchin).

NOT NORMAL: One of the president's informal advisers, Gingrich, calling for the jailing of someone who spoke out against the president.

JANUARY 26, 2017: MORE NORMAL VERSUS NOT NORMAL

OK, another edition of NORMAL versus NOT NORMAL. Keeping in mind again that "normal" is not good, just what we would expect a Republican president to do.

NORMAL: Reversing course on the Dakota Access and Keystone Pipelines.

NOT NORMAL: Initiating (or saying) you will initiate a voter-fraud investigation in the absence of any evidence of a meaningful amount of voter fraud.

NORMAL: Reexamining the previous administration's policy on admitting refugees.

NOT NORMAL: Essentially deciding who you are going to admit on the basis of religion (at least according to the drafts of the executive orders I've seen).

NORMAL: Telling career staff not to talk to the press.

NOT NORMAL: Suspending ongoing grants and contracts, and deleting web pages with factual information. (Unclear: social media, this is new ground.)

NOT NORMAL: Threatening to send troops into Chicago.

NOT NORMAL: Giving a rambling interview that one person described as seeming more like an interview of a mental patient who believes he is president.

JANUARY 28, 2017: THE TRAVEL BAN (ORIGINALLY APPEARED IN THE *HILL*)[6]

Sometimes government actions result in making the problem they are trying to fix worse rather than solving it.

For example, we don't know much yet about the harm of smoking e-cigarettes. But we are relatively sure that they are less harmful than regular cigarettes. Efforts to make e-cigarettes more difficult to purchase therefore hold the risk of increasing the number of people consuming regular cigarettes and thereby increasing the risk of lung cancer.

Risk assessors often describe these as "risk-risk trade-offs."

Another example a risk-risk trade-off comes from the world of automobile emissions. When new standards for tailpipe emissions are set, they apply only to new cars (reasonably so, since retrofitting old cars would be very expensive). This increases the price of new cars. The increased price leads potential buyers to hold on to their old polluting cars longer, and therefore the level of pollution (at least in the short run) is higher than it would be without the new requirement.

President Trump's new executive order on immigration may be a classic example of a risk-risk trade-off. It targets two groups of individuals: refugees and those from seven countries (Iran, Iraq, Libya, Somalia,

---

6 Stuart Shapiro, "Trump's Refugee Ban is the Perfect ISIS Recruiting Tool," *The Hill*, January 28, 2017, http://thehill.com/blogs/pundits-blog/homeland-security/316697-trumps-refugee-ban-is-the-perfect-isis-recruiting-tool.

Sudan, Syria, and Yemen). Based on available data, members of neither of these groups represent a significant risk of committing a terrorist attack.

There have been three terrorist crimes committed by refugees since September 11. As ThinkProgress notes, "Two of the men were indicted and jailed for plotting to send weapons to terrorist organizations in Iraq. One Uzbek man was convicted of terrorism-related charges for possessing explosives and supporting a terrorist organization in Uzbekistan."

The vetting procedures for refugees put in place by the Obama administration make attacks even less likely. As for the seven countries from which we are going to suspend immigration, there have been no terrorist attacks on American soil by visa holders from those countries.

Where have terrorists in recent years come from? Whether it is in San Bernardino, California, where the attack was by a lawful permanent resident from Pakistan or Fort Hood, Texas, and Orlando, Florida, where the shooters were native-born Americans, the terrorists were already here—they were not recent immigrants. They were mentally unstable individuals who were radicalized by anti-US rhetoric from terrorist organizations like Al-Qaeda and the Islamic State in Iraq and Syria (ISIS).

Well, guess who just got some amazing fodder for their anti-US rhetoric? As Sen. Chris Murphy (D-Conn.) has said, the executive order has given ISIS a "path to rebirth." An organization that was on the run in Syria and Iraq has just been handed an amazing recruiting tool: a written proclamation from the US president that everything they've been saying all these years about the United States being at war with Muslims is true.

This recruiting tool is likely to be effective in messages consumed by individuals like those who perpetrated the awful attacks in Fort Hood, Orlando, and San Bernardino. So while we will be keeping out individuals who mean the United States no harm and indeed are in many cases the victims of those who do, we will have handed our enemies an important weapon.

By allegedly trying to decrease the risk of a terrorist attack, we may have increased it.

JANUARY 29, 2017: TRUMP THREATENS THE COURTS OVER THEIR SUSPENSION OF HIS TRAVEL BAN

In 1832, Chief Justice John Marshall issued a ruling on tribal sovereignty. President Andrew Jackson (whom Trump has taken as a role model) is reported to have said "John Marshall has made his decision, now let him enforce it." The quote may be apocryphal, but Jackson did largely ignore Marshall's order. This is where we are headed. Everything in the past thirty-six hours counts as NOT NORMAL (unless 1832 is your baseline).

FEBRUARY 1, 2017: TRUMP NOMINATES NEIL GORSUCH TO THE SUPREME COURT

Normal: A Republican president nominating a very conservative justice (described as a Scalia clone).

Not Normal: There being a vacancy because the Senate refused to even consider the nomination of the previous president.

The nomination should be filibustered. And rather than letting conservatives call the seat, "Scalia's seat" we should call it "Garland's seat."

FEBRUARY 2, 2017: TRUMP DOESN'T KNOW WHO FREDERICK DOUGLAS IS

It just occurred to me. Donald Trump's monologue on Frederick Douglas (not normal) is exactly how a report from Bill and Ted would have sounded.

FEBRUARY 5, 2017: TRUMP CONTINUES TO HARANGUE THE COURTS

A very not normal weekend. Trump's tweets about how judges will be held responsible if there is a terrorist attack and his praise of Putin are of one piece. He might as well just complete the thought and say, "Judges in Russia wouldn't dare do this."

FEBRUARY 7, 2017: TWO WEEK STATUS REPORT

I can't keep up! In the past two days, Trump has cited underreported attacks (White House spelling) in Paris, Orlando, and San Bernardino,

Melania sued to preserve her ability to make money off the First Lady's position, and Trump freaked out about Melissa McCarthy playing Sean Spicer on SNL. All of that and the *Times* article revealing the dysfunction in the White House.

So where are we now?

We have a president who is essentially a spoiled child. He is petulant, ignorant, and spiteful. These are bad characteristics in a dictator and worse ones in a president. He has no real sense of how American government works and is most concerned with settling scores and having high poll ratings to feed his narcissism. With no goals and no purpose besides self-aggrandizement, this leaves him open to manipulation by his advisers.

There seems to be a battle afoot for that manipulation. Bannon represents the "not normal." He wants to establish an authoritarian state (remember he admires Lenin) based on white supremacy. He knows he has to move fast because (a) Trump may implode at any moment and (b) once they get their deregulation and tax cuts, the Republicans may throw Trump overboard. Of course, Bannon is weakened every time Trump sees him portrayed as the brains of the operation. Still his whispers about autocracy and white supremacy must resonate with Trump.

On the other side of the battle is Priebus (reprehensible but normal). Priebus wants to keep Trump acting like a typical Republican and keep him popular enough so that Republicans in Congress can do their dirty work. It wouldn't surprise me if Priebus is in regular contact with Ryan and Pence and is working to undermine Bannon.

The *Times* article portrays a level of incompetence that gives one hope that this administration will collapse in on itself. Unfortunately, in the meantime, sh&t happens. Iran denounces us for our anti-Muslim policies from the moral high ground. Putin kills critics. Le Pen announces in France with a very Trumpian flair. A German newspaper contemplates an anti-American alliance. This is two weeks. Four years is unimaginable.

FEBRUARY 11, 2017: BACK TO THE SCENARIOS

Last month I outlined four possible scenarios for a Trump presidency. For those of you that didn't see it.

1. Pressure leads Republicans to impeachment hearings.
2. A crisis leads Republicans to impeachment hearings.
3. Trump successfully establishes an autocracy.
4. Trump governs as a typical Republican.

We are now three weeks into the Trump administration. Where do we stand? First I'd add a fifth scenario (Nate Silver has fourteen; see first comment). We have chaos. We go from crisis to crisis on a daily basis. The United States loses prestige quickly as allies look elsewhere for support. Domestically bad things happen (like yesterday's ICE raids), but the lasting damage is to faith in democracy as the opposition gets exhausted. Trump survives his term, but the United States is in dire shape in 2020. Jeb Bush called Trump the chaos candidate and may end up being remembered for that phrase.

If I were going to rank the scenarios in likelihood now, I'd go 2, 3, 5, 4, 1. The two things I had wrong were that I underestimated the cravenness of Republicans in Congress (a more generous person would call it political responsiveness, but I'm in no mood to be generous) and the sheer insanity of Trump (which says something since I thought he was crazy). The increased likelihood of a major crisis stems largely from his being mentally unhinged.

FEBRUARY 14, 2017: THE REVELATIONS ABOUT MICHAEL FLYNN EMERGE

A few of you have asked me about impeachment and constitutional crises. The first thing to remember is that impeachment is a *political* decision, not a *legal* one. In 1970, then House Minority Leader Gerald R. Ford defined the criterion as he saw it: "An impeachable offense is whatever a majority of the House of Representatives considers it to be at a given moment in history." Legal setbacks can set the stage for impeachment, but the decision to start an investigation that could lead to legal problems and the decision to act on those findings are political. You need ten to fifteen Republican senators to want to investigate and fifty to seventy Republicans in the House to want to impeach once the findings of that investigation become public. Right now the political conditions do not favor impeachment. Could they? How do we get there? I can see three current issues mushrooming, but only consider one reasonably likely, in decreasing order of likelihood.

1. Russia. Here's what we know. Flynn called Russia during the transition. The call was about lifting sanctions. Russia hacked the DNC e-mails during the election. None of those will lead to impeachment. But…if Trump knew about the hacks or the Flynn calls, then we have something. Now after Flynn's resignation, the questions are these: (1) Will Flynn angrily talk? and (2) What else do the intelligence agencies have? The biggest reason this could lead to impeachment is that there are senators who worry about Russia and may be ready to move forward with an investigation before Trump's approval ratings tank. Probability of investigation before 2018 midterms: 40 percent (up from thirty last night). Probability of impeachment before 2018 midterms: 10 percent (up from five last night).

2. Corruption. Trump and his family have almost certainly already violated federal laws and possibly the emoluments clause of the Constitution. So why isn't this higher? People don't seem to care. This is the one that is probably most dependent on Trump's approval ratings. As long as they are above thirty or so, I can't see anyone moving forward on his use of Mar-a-Lago for state events or his weekends (which the taxpayers reimburse him $3 million per weekend for), the Trump kids expanding their business, or Ivanka hawking her brands. But if his approval drops and Republicans begin to fret about their electoral chances, then maybe they will all of sudden find that these things bother them. Probability of investigation before 2018 midterms: 10 percent. Probability of impeachment before 2018 midterms: 2 percent.

3. Defying a judge (on something besides corruption or Russia). CBP acted as if judges hadn't suspended the refugee order for a while with no repercussions. This is a signal. If Trump defies judges in ways that are popular with his base, I don't think Republicans in

Congress have the spine to buck him (and many may agree with him). Again approval ratings make a difference, but this is also issue specific. As much as it bothers those of us on the left, acting illegally against Muslims (particularly if there is another attack—which of course would improve Trump's ratings) isn't gonna get Trump impeached. Probability of investigation before 2018 midterms: 1 percent. Probability of impeachment before 2018 midterms: <1 percent.

The one other factor to consider though is the sheer incompetence demonstrated thus far by the administration. The Flynn imbroglio is one part evil, four parts idiocy. They could blunder their way into a crisis.

FEBRUARY 17, 2017: TRUMP VERSUS THE INTELLIGENCE AGENCIES

Intelligence agencies appear to be taking a bigger and bigger role in the battle against Trump. Memes and rumors have circulated about how intelligence agents have sworn revenge against Trump and claimed that Trump will "die in jail."

I admit that image is appealing right now. But I think we need to think about our reaction to this front in the battle. Many of us recoiled when FBI Director Comey announced that the investigation of Hillary Clinton was reopening (probably in response to the fact that FBI agents were likely to leak this information). There are some differences, of course, but both involve a law-enforcement or intelligence agency wading into political waters (the Trumpites of course loved it when the FBI came in but are crying foul now).

We need to be very careful here. Two years ago if anyone told a progressive that intelligence agencies would try to bring down a president, we would have recoiled. Ask any progressive of a certain age about their feelings about J. Edgar Hoover, for example. Having to rely on the "deep state" (by the way, a very ambiguous and loaded term that generally means any part of government we don't like—conservatives consider the bureaucracy [IRS or EPA, etc.] the deep state) means we are in dire times.

So my hope that if the intelligence agencies have damning material on Trump and they use this material to its maximal effectiveness comes from the feeling that these are indeed dire times. His presidency gets worse by the day (yesterday's press conference remarkably set a new low—this weekend's Nuremburg rally is going to be worse), and it feels like an existential crisis. But the intelligence agencies undermining his presidency are not a good thing. It's just less of a bad thing than where we are headed now.

One other side note: There is no guarantee that the intelligence agencies will win this battle; Trump and his allies have their weapons as well—Cheney and Rumsfeld were very successful in manipulating the intelligence agencies toward their goals. Fortunately, Trump does not seem to have any bureaucratic infighters who could hold a candle to Cheney or Rumsfeld.

FEBRUARY 20, 2017: TRUMP OR PENCE?

Several of you have asked me in the past week if (in the still unlikely but growing chance) Trump gets impeached, would Pence be worse? The short answer is no.

The long answer of course is more complicated. Pence would doubtlessly be more effective in passing legislation and issuing regulations that enact policies inimical to many of us. This would particularly be true in any "honeymoon period" where the devout Pence talks about "healing" the rifts of the Trump impeachment.

And as a well-to-do white straight male, keep in mind that these policies, while they would deeply offend my moral sensibilities, would have little material effect upon me. Understand that there is no way for me to separate that fact from my answer to this question.

There are three areas though where Pence will undoubtedly be better than Trump, and I think those trump (pun intended) the downsides. The first is that a major war that begins either through US action or through misinterpretation by allies or enemies of the mixed signals of a Trump administration becomes much less likely under Pence.

Second, the likelihood that we retain a free press, freedom of speech, and free and fair elections are much greater under a President Pence.

Trump clearly values none of these things, and while he has taken no successful steps to curtail these rights yet, he definitely wants to. President Pence will peacefully hand over power to the next president, be it Warren, Kaine, Kasich, or Rubio.

Finally, Pence will not actively stir up hatred of other groups the way Trump and his white-supremacist allies have. Policies that implement discrimination are insidious. But the hatred that Trump has made people feel safe expressing is worse. A Trump impeachment would begin the long process of putting that back in the box it was in and eventually figuring out how to kill it.

In short, the changes that Pence would make are reversible (extreme but "normal"). The potential changes that Trump would make are not (reversible or normal).

FEBRUARY 24, 2017: EXCLUDING THE PRESS

Very Not Normal: Excluding news organizations from White House press briefings because they report things you don't like. Not very surprising though. Authoritarian regimes know that the first step in consolidating power is to control the press. One way is flood alternative sources with false information; the other is what we saw today.

FEBRUARY 26, 2017: A GOOD DAY

Lately I've been posting mostly negative things. The past thirty-six hours have had three positive developments that bear noting.

1. The Democrats won a special election that gave them control of the Delaware State Senate. Seems trivial, right? Well, it's not earth shattering, but three months after Trump's victory, the Democrats took a seat that they won in 2014 by two points by seventeen points.

2. Darrell Issa, Republican Congressman from California, called for a special prosecutor to investigate Trump's ties to Russia. Issa, typically a huge partisan, won his seat 51–49 in 2016 in a district Clinton carried handily. He has been rated the most vulnerable GOP incumbent in 2018.

3. The Democrats now have two very good people in charge of the DNC. They are both very progressive and have a strategic vision for the campaigns ahead. While the DNC chair is an overrated position in terms of its importance, the symbolism of having a Hispanic and a Muslim in charge of the party at a time when these are the two groups most specifically targeted by the Republican president is a good thing.

The first two of these developments come straight from the energy that Trump's election has given to Democrats. They happened because people have protested, donated money, showed up at town halls, and called their representatives. Keep it up.

MARCH 1, 2017: THE STATE OF THE UNION

When a "not normal" president gives a speech that approaches "normal" resist the tendency to praise it. If anyone else who has ever served in that office gave last night's speech, he would have been roundly criticized.

MARCH 2, 2017: TRUMP-RUSSIA BEGINS TO HEAT UP

Within an hour last night, two huge Russia-related stories broke. The first by the *Washington Post* revealed that AG Sessions talked to the Russian ambassador during the campaign after claiming otherwise under oath. While no one wants to see Trump's worst cabinet pick suffer more than I do (Jefferson Beauregard Sessions III—is there a name that screams plantation owner more loudly?), I suspect that over the long run, the more important story was broken by the *Times*.

The *Times* reported that the Obama administration spent its last month spreading the intelligence about Russia, the election, and Trump far and wide. This will make it much harder for the Trump administration to suppress this info. In fact, it wouldn't surprise me if the Sessions story broke as the result of this effort.

We still don't know how serious the accusations might be. There has been no public release about the substance of the communications between Trump campaign folks and Russia. Someone on Twitter last week said that this feels like 1973–74 compressed into a few weeks though. Like Watergate, we need someone to flip or a tape to emerge before one can talk realistically about impeachment. If it does, this ends in impeachment or dictatorship. But until it does, we have the drip, drip of revelations like the Sessions one.

MARCH 4, 2017: TRUMP ACCUSES OBAMA OF WIRETAPPING HIM

A few thoughts on this morning's tweetstorm.

In case you missed it, Trump sent out a series of tweets this morning accusing President Obama of illegally wiretapping him.

1. Presidents can't order wiretaps (a restriction put in place after Nixon I believe). If there was a wiretap, it was ordered by DOJ and approved by a FISA court. It means there was some cause for it. Trump could show his innocence by declassifying the order for the wiretap. If it exists…

2. The other alternative, which I wouldn't dismiss, is that Trump is simply making crap up again. Throughout the campaign whenever he was accused of something, he said Hillary did it but was worse ("you're the puppet" being the most memorable example). Here he accuses Obama of Nixon like activities right after the Sessions imbroglio led to the most prominent set of Watergate analogies.

3. A half hour after these tweets, he tweeted about (wait for it, drum roll) Schwarzenegger and *Celebrity Apprentice*. He is nuts.

4. There are two things one can take out of these tweets, either (a) he is the subject of a major investigation or (b) he's batsh%t crazy. They aren't mutually exclusive.

MARCH 7, 2017: DISTRACTION

Don't get distracted by Ben Carson calling slaves immigrants; he's a moron. The Republicans in the House yesterday proposed a replacement for Obamacare that would take health insurance away from fifteen million people.

Don't get distracted by a House health-care plan that will never pass the Senate; Donald Trump continues to use the presidency to profit from Mar a Lago.

Don't get distracted by Trump's Florida resort; he continues to assert that he was wiretapped by Obama despite Comey's insistence otherwise. He's encouraging Congress to investigate Obama, not Putin.

Don't get distracted by Trump's clearly false allegations. He just reinstated his travel ban, and the changes are largely cosmetic; it is still a Muslim ban, and ICE will likely enforce it the way they did the previous ban.

Don't get distracted by Trump's travel ban…

Screw it; just don't get distracted. We're being governed by a madman who is supported by Nazis and is being enabled by venal hacks. Everything is important now (OK, except maybe Carson—where did they find this guy?).

MARCH 9, 2017: TRUMP'S GUIDANCE ON IMMIGRATION ENFORCEMENT (ORIGINALLY APPEARED IN THE *HILL*)[7]

Well, that didn't take long. After years of complaining about President Obama using executive powers to usurp the law, President Trump's Department of Homeland Security (DHS) issued guidance late last month that looks a lot like all the actions that candidate Trump and his supporters criticized. The guidance instructs immigration enforcement personnel to expand their priorities in detaining and deporting undocumented immigrants.

In other words, it is the executive branch changing policy on its own.

There are two ways of looking at the legal status of this guidance document. Both ways are problematic for the Trump administration. The more problematic is that it is a violation of the Administrative Procedure Act (APA). Under this interpretation, DHS should have issued a regulation and accepted public comment. Agencies issue guidance documents

---

7 Stuart Shapiro, "White House Immigration Guidance is Executive Overreach," *The Hill*, March 9, 2017, http://thehill.com/blogs/pundits-blog/immigration/ 323118-white-house-immigration-guidance-is-executive-overreach.

frequently, and many have argued that they do this to avoid the requirements of the APA and other procedures they are required to follow when issuing a regulation.

The legal status of guidance documents is a contested question and probably should vary from circumstance to circumstance. But many of those who have most loudly criticized these documents as executive branch overreach are defenders of the current occupant of the Oval Office. They certainly criticized President Obama's use of guidance to reset immigration enforcement priorities as unconstitutional or illegal.

While they move in the opposite direction, Trump's instructions are the same type of action as the one taken by Obama.

Even if the use of a guidance document rather than a regulation to implement such a large policy change is legitimate, there are still problems with it. DHS ignored numerous requirements within the executive branch for guidance documents, such as those issued by the Office of Management and Budget (OMB).

For example, "economically significant guidance documents"—those that have an impact of more than $100 million—are required by OMB to be put out for public comment like regulations under the APA. Any credible economic analysis will likely show that the impact of this order is greater than this threshold—just the cost of hiring of the additional customs agents, alone, will exceed it.

But DHS did not put this guidance out for public comment.

Finally, the recent executive order requiring agencies to find offsets for regulatory costs appears to have been ignored in this instance. The OMB bulletin implementing the order says that OMB has discretion to require cost offsets for guidance documents.

Did the OMB review the new DHS guidance? Given what are likely very large costs for the US economy from deporting millions of immigrants, why wasn't DHS asked to find ways to offset these costs?

No one should be surprised, however, that President Trump failed to follow these requirements curbing executive power—even the one he put in place himself two weeks ago. Presidents in general tend to try to expand their power to the largest extent possible. And this president seems particularly interested in maximizing executive authority.

As always, with a compliant Congress, it will be up to the courts to rein in the president and his agencies.

MARCH 11, 2017: TIME FOR SOME NORMAL VERSUS NOT NORMAL

- NORMAL: Putting in place your preferred people in the US attorney's office.
- NOT NORMAL: Giving all the US attorneys one day's notice and thereby gutting any pending investigations (and if one of these investigations is of the president or his associates, this moves into *very, very* NOT NORMAL territory).
- NORMAL: Following through on one of your campaign pledges by putting forth a proposal that repeals your predecessor's health-care legislation.
- NOT NORMAL: Rushing it through Congress with limited hearings and before the Congressional Budget Office can "score" it. And demeaning CBO in an attempt to damage their credibility. (I am of mixed feelings about whether the Republican plan will pass. I lean no, but many I respect differ. In any case, when you make your regular call to your representative, this should be at the top of your list.)

The allegations this past week about various Trump aides are in various stages of being proven. But the stink surrounding Roger Stone, Michael Flynn, Carter Paige, and Paul Manafort is definitely NOT NORMAL. Let's just hope that there are enough people left investigating these potentially treasonous actions to go public before things get too much worse (to see how bad they could be, read this[8] on Sessions/Bannon/Miller).

---

8 Emily Bazelon, "Department of Justification," *New York Times*, February 28, 2017, https://www.nytimes.com/2017/02/28/magazine/jeff-sessions-stephen-bannon-justice-department.html?_r=1

MARCH 15, 2017: ATTACKING OBJECTIVITY

Was going to write a *Hill* column on this, but Steve Benen beat me to it and probably did it better than I would have.[9]

The basic point is this, the attacks this week on the Congressional Budget Office as being wrong about its claim that twenty-four million will be uninsured, on BLS for manipulating unemployment numbers for Obama, and the continued denial of climate science are all of one piece. The Trump administration wants us to not believe anything we hear. If nothing is credible, then anything is credible. Claiming Obama wiretapped Trump becomes as believable as saying the planet is getting warmer.

This is not a new technique. Orwell wrote about it. Putin practices it. Truth is what the dear leader says it is. You shouldn't trust anything else. And in an age of news sources that really are fake and the flood of information that we are all faced with, it is easy to begin to doubt. Furthermore, there is fundamental uncertainty in all social science (and science too). Maybe twenty-two million will lose health insurance. Maybe twenty-six million. But this uncertainty shouldn't obscure the central point that a lot of people will lose health insurance.

Organizations that have long developed reputations for credibility like CBO and BLS and institutions like science need our help more than ever. They will make mistakes. But they are the best we have. And the information they give you is far better than the information Trump and his folks will give you (or that your favorite renegade website will give you).

MARCH 17, 2017: TRUMP'S FIRST BUDGET

A statement of priorities.

As most of you know, yesterday, President Trump submitted his budget to Congress. That, of course, is NORMAL. It is also normal for Congress to make massive changes to the president's submission in the seven-eight months between submission and passage. This is less common when the

---

9 Steve Benen, "As Health Care Debate Intensifies, GOP Takes Aim at Empiricism," *The Maddow Blog*, March 14, 2017, http://www.msnbc.com/rachel-maddow-show/health-care-debate-intensifies-gop-takes-aim-empiricism.

same party controls Congress and the presidency. But the relationship between the GOP in Congress and this president is not yet NORMAL.

So we don't know which of Trump's cruel heartless cuts will actually become law. Unfortunately some will. But I see the primary importance of yesterday's budget submission as revealing what this administration cares about. When you do your family budget, you are saying what you care about. For those of us in the middle class and higher, that means vacation versus home improvements, eating out versus organic foods, and so on. Your budget says something about you (and yes for many people, a budget means food vs. medicine vs. electricity—this says less about them and more about their circumstances of course).

Trump (and the reprehensible Mick Mulvaney) is saying he cares about (a) the military and (b) his wall. He doesn't care about the poor, the sick, science, the environment, workers, diplomacy, and the list goes on. The extent of his proposed cuts is NOT NORMAL. No one should ever let his voters forget that this is what their leader cares about (maybe they feel the same way—I sadly suspect more of them do than those of us in our bubble think, but some were hoodwinked—the reveal was yesterday).

MARCH 19, 2017: SCENARIO UPDATE

Twice I have outlined five possible scenarios for the Trump presidency. To avoid asking you to scroll through my way too cluttered time line, they were (1) slow march to impeachment, (2) unexpected disaster leads to impeachment, (3) the erosion of democracy, (4) typical Republican president, and (5) chaos as we lurch from one minor crisis to another.

The original order of probability was 1–5. Now I am thinking 5, 1, 3, 2, 4. In part that is because of the inner chaos in the Trump administration characterized the *Washington Post* article below.[10] Basically there is war between Bannon (who wants scenario 3), who is allied with Priebus

---

10 Philip Rucker and Robert Costa, "Inside Trump's White House, New York Moderates Spark Infighting and Suspicion," *Washington Post*, March 18, 2017, https://www.washingtonpost.com/politics/inside-trumps-white-house-new-york-moderates-spark-infighting-and-suspicion/2017/03/18/51e3c4d2-0b1c-11e7-a15f-a58d4a988474_story.html?utm_term=.b8b92b95b168.

(who wants 4), and Kushner (who wants 6—a socially liberal kleptocracy—which ain't gonna happen).

The chaos is a direct function of Trump's leadership. He doesn't believe anything (except in making money, his own brilliance, and in the superiority of white males). Therefore, he can careen from point of view to point of view without compunction. Republicans therefore have no idea where he will be from day to day on issues or what he will tweet out, soaking up the oxygen they need to enact their agendas.

The problem with predicting scenario 5 is that it is by definition not stable. Instead of a minor crisis, we could have a major one (leading to scenario 2 or 3)—like North Korea threatening Seoul or Tokyo. One of the sides within the White House could gain ascendancy (moving us to scenario 3 or 4). But until that happens, it is very hard to foresee what will emerge from the chaos.

One caveat, the testimony of Comey this week could move us back to scenario one being preeminent.

MARCH 21, 2017: WHEN NO NEWS IS BIG NEWS

The Comey hearings yesterday deservedly received a lot of media (and social media) attention. But did we learn anything new? Not really. The two key takeaways from the hearings are as follows:

1. The FBI is investigating links between the Trump campaign and Russia.
2. President Obama did not order a wiretap of candidate Trump.

If you are paying attention to the news (and I know most of you are), the logical response to these two items is "Well, duh."

But still the headlines are merited. Why? Because the FBI is investigating a sitting president on charges that could lead to accusations of treason. No matter how many times you hear that, you should be reminded yet again that this is NOT NORMAL.

Will they find anything? I don't know. But Senator Feinstein says that Trump will resign shortly (I think that's crazy but still…). Rep. Nunes acted like a panicked child in trying to defend the Trump administration. (His claim that he had never heard of Stone or Manafort rivals my nine-year-old screaming that he didn't do something when we saw him do it, same for Spicey's claim that Manafort didn't really have a big role on the campaign when Manafort was the campaign manager.) All of these news stories plus the continued existence (and possible eventual testimony) of Manafort, Stone, Paige, and Flynn tell you that this story isn't going away.

MARCH 22, 2017: CBO ANALYZES THE HOUSE HEALTH-CARE BILL (ORIGINALLY APPEARED IN THE *HILL*)[11]

For the past seven years, I have run a master's in public policy (MPP) program. Each year, as we teach the students basic research methods, microeconomics, program evaluation, and benefit-cost analysis, I hear one question over and over again: "Will anyone use the work we do, or is it *all politics?*"

Never has that question been harder to answer than in the highly polarized and politicized climate of the past year.

Recently, however, those of us who advocate for good analysis in government got some encouraging news. The Congressional Budget Office (CBO) published an estimate of the impacts of the Republican health-care legislation being debated in the House of Representatives (a.k.a. "RyanCare" or "TrumpCare"). The CBO produced its analysis in a remarkably short period of time. The agency estimated that twenty-four million people would lose health insurance and that premiums for insurance plans would eventually drop.

The terms of the debate on the health-care legislation changed immediately. Gone were the empty claims that no one would lose their health insurance as a result of this legislation.

While the CBO estimate of twenty-four million is indeed just an estimate, and the exact number of people who would lose health insurance is

---

11 Stuart Shapiro, "CBO's Healthcare Report Shows the Value of Good Analysis," *The Hill*, March 22, 2017, http://thehill.com/blogs/pundits-blog/healthcare/325180-cbos-healthcare-report-shows-value-of-good-analysis.

uncertain, the CBO leaves no question that the number is far, far greater than zero. In fact, the publication of the CBO report led to a leak that the president's own staff estimated the number as twenty-six million.

Now the defenders of the bill, such as Speaker Paul Ryan (R-Wis.), have had to change their argument regarding its impacts. Ryan now argues that the bill will increase freedom and choice for Americans (well, at least for those who can still afford health insurance).

Now the policy question in the bill is correctly framed. Is it worth depriving millions of access to health insurance in order to increase the freedom to choose not to buy health insurance for others?

This trade-off is a fundamentally political question. We use politics to solve questions of redistribution within society. The Republican health-care plan, as made clear by the CBO report, is a redistribution of welfare from older sicker people to younger healthy ones.

It may very well be that this bill or (more likely) a modified version of it passes Congress. But if this takes place, those who vote for it will be telling their constituents that they are OK with this redistribution.

If the bill fails because Republicans do not feel comfortable voting for this trade-off, the CBO analysis will be a big part of the reason. If the bill is modified to soften the blow on recipients of Medicaid or others hurt by the legislation, the CBO analysis will be a big part of the reason.

And the next time my students ask whether policy analysis or economics can make a difference, I will have a new example to give them.

MARCH 23, 2017: HOW TO FOLLOW THE HEALTH-CARE VOTE

Right now I can see today's vote in the House unfolding in four ways.

1. Ryan pulls the bill. This is the best possible outcome. It will signify that Ryan has decided that he can't put together a bill that has enough votes to pass. It probably kills health-care reform for the near future and is a big blow to Ryan.
2. Ryan delays the bill for a week or less. This means that Ryan doesn't yet have the votes but thinks that a majority is within reach.

3. The bill passes with additions that may run afoul of "reconcili-
    ation rules" in the Senate. The bill is now crafted so that only a
    majority is needed in the Senate. It's complicated, but this means
    that only budget-related provisions can be included. This scenario
    would allow Republicans to blame the Senate Parliamentarian and
    Democrats for the ultimate failure of the bill. This is what I think
    will happen today.
4. The bill passes without such provisions. Still very much in play. It
    is not clear whether such a bill could get a majority in the Senate.

If you have a Republican representative, call and tell him or her to oppose
the bill in any form.

MARCH 26, 2017: ON CONSPIRACY THEORIES

I don't like conspiracy theories. Often randomness or incompetence is far
better explanation for why things happen. It's particularly important to
avoid conspiracy theories when they support your preexisting beliefs.

But I have to admit, this one is growing on me. The tweetstorm below[12]
describes a series of meetings at the Mayflower Hotel this past summer
between the Trump campaign and Russian operatives. The first one in the
comments sums up what we know about Michael Flynn. There are rumors
(yes, just rumors) that Flynn may be talking to the FBI.

The unproven parts of this theory are explosive beyond belief. Trump
getting a financial payoff from the Russians. Sessions still not disclosing
all of his meetings with Kislyak, Trump campaign knowledge of the DNC
hack. Watergate would indeed be a footnote compared to this if true. I
don't know if it is true.

But the parts that we do know: Russia hacking the DNC, Flynn's multiple meetings with Kislyak and his accepting payments from both Russia
and Turkey, Manafort's connections to Yanukovych, Stone tweeting out
about the Podesta e-mails before Wikileaks published them, Tillerson

---

12 Seth Abrahamson's tweet storm can be found here: https://twitter.com/
SethAbramson/status/845089192438829056.

pulling out of NATO meetings, and the recent spurt of murders of people who have crossed Putin are enough to be very concerned and to demand investigations.

We won on healthcare this week. But meanwhile, more than one hundred civilians were allegedly bombed by us in Iraq possibly as a result of a strategy of taking the "handcuffs off the military." Every day this administration is in office is a day closer to potential disaster. If this material is true, it needs to be brought out as soon as possible and would be the biggest NOT NORMAL of all. If it isn't, there is now plenty of time to fight the other NORMALs (like tax reform, environmental policy, etc.). When you call your senators this week and tell them to oppose Gorsuch, tell them to demand an independent investigation too.

MARCH 28, 2017: FILIBUSTERING A QUALIFIED NOMINEE

First, some history. Antonin Scalia was confirmed 98–0. Ruth Bader Ginsburg was confirmed 96–3. So it hasn't always been this way, even after the contentious Bork hearings in 1987 (Scalia's vote was before then, but Ginsburg's was afterward). The increased partisanship that broadly affects our elected officials has taken a dire toll on Supreme Court nominations.

Both Merrick Garland and Neil Gorsuch are qualified to be on the Supreme Court. In an earlier age, both would have been confirmed with little fanfare. But in my view, the move last year to not allow a vote on Garland was a step change that needs to be dealt with before confirming Gorsuch.

An eye for an eye and the whole world goes blind? Perhaps. But as long as the Republicans are more willing to up the ante on confirmations than the Democrats, then the Democrats will have a permanent disadvantage. It is possible that the Republicans will get rid of the filibuster of Supreme Court nominations in response to a Democratic filibuster of Gorsuch. If so, we roll the dice on the health of Ginsburg and Kennedy. Remember that if a Democrat wins in 2020, Republican may quickly regret the end of the filibuster (as Democrats now do for cabinet confirmations).

But if the Democrats allow the confirmation of Gorsuch while getting nothing in return, then we are still rolling the dice on the health of

Ginsburg and Kennedy. Nothing would stop the same brinksmanship in the next confirmation battle. The time to fight is now.

I called my senator this morning and told him to support the filibuster.

MARCH 31, 2017: NIXON AND TRUMP

I've been thinking about Richard Nixon lately. I started rewatching the *American Experience* documentary about him (maybe for the fifth time, but it has been a while). Then I saw this book review in the *Times* yesterday.[13]

As the review makes clear, the parallels between Nixon and Trump are numerous. There's the racism, the paranoia, the hatred of the press, and the demonizing of elites while also wanting their approval. Trump's appeal to "real Americans" parallels Nixon's to the silent majority and the "forgotten man." Trump's emphasis on crime is lifted straight from Nixon. It makes sense that they might both end up disgraced in scandals that only a paranoid narcissist could be convinced to participate in.

But there are differences too. Nixon came from poverty; his father was a failed lemon farmer. This doesn't excuse his later resentments, but it makes him a bit more sympathetic than the bonus baby currently in the White House. Also, Nixon was much smarter and understood how government worked. He graduated third in his class at Duke Law. He spent a life in government. During his presidency he signed the bills that created EPA and OSHA, started detente with Russia, and met with Mao (and yes, did lots of awful, awful things especially indiscriminately bombing Southeast Asia). Maybe that explains why it took six years to bring him down, whereas Trump is already foundering.

I guess what I'm getting at: Donald Trump has all the bad qualities of perhaps the worst president in US history (or at least one of the three or four worst) and none of the good ones.

---

13 Jennifer Senior, "'Richard Nixon,' Portrait of a Thin-Skinned Media-Hating President," *New York Times*, March 29, 2017, https://www.nytimes.com/2017/03/29/books/richard-nixon-biography-john-a-farrell.html?_r=0.

APRIL 5, 2017: THE WORLD TURNED UPSIDE DOWN

With Trump's domestic agenda largely stalled (except for brutal enforcement against immigrants and lack of enforcement against corporations and police departments), it can be tempting to chortle at the failed start to the presidency. But to do so, would be to stop one's gaze at the nation's borders.

Between the combination of incompetence (see Trump's statement on Syria and Tillerson's on North Korea) and ill will, Trump is already having profound and deleterious effects around the world. Giving the military freer rein to drop bombs will inevitably increase civilian casualties and serve as a recruiting tool for ISIS and Al-Qaeda. Embracing General Sisi of Egypt tells dissenters there that America will not stand up for them and implicitly gives the same message to dissenters everywhere (Turkey, the Philippines, etc.).

And Trump hasn't faced a real international test yet. What happens when anti-ISIS forces take Raqqa and the Turks and Kurds begin disputing who gets the city? What happens when North Korea begins threatening to use its nuclear arsenal? Jared Kushner will solve it?

Like it or not, the United States is the indispensable nation. When we wiggle a pinky, the world reacts. When we coddle a dictator, freedom and liberty everywhere suffer. One of the biggest reasons to be rooting for or pushing impeachment is that the consequences for the world of four years of the combination of incompetence and maliciousness that Trump has thus far shown are profound.

APRIL 7, 2017: TRUMP BOMBS SYRIA

I don't know what the right action regarding Syria's reprehensible gassing of its own citizens is.

I do know that I don't trust this administration to come up with it.

Two other quick notes:

- If the Trump administration action stops with last night's fifty missiles, then the response is quite NORMAL. If it escalates, then that's another story.

- While NORMAL, the bombing is most likely illegal. But no one will do anything about it. Also NORMAL.

APRIL 9, 2017: MORE THOUGHTS ON SYRIA

David Frum writes a nice piece[14] on the problems with Trump's decision to bomb Syrian airfields Thursday night. If another president (say Obama or Bush Sr.) had done the same thing, I would feel confident that he had weighed a series of options, discussed the risk with advisers, and informed key allies. I don't feel confident that any of that has been done.

Even more worrisome than the points made by Frum though is that I am pretty confident that Trump will learn very dangerous lessons from this. Faced with declining approval ratings, Trump secured rare bipartisan praise for his actions. Trump is not a complex thinker. He is going to absorb the lesson of "drop bombs, get applause." This means more bombs are coming. Yemen? Or more worrisome, the Korean Peninsula?

Many of those praising Trump were careful to couch their language with statements about the need to consult in the future or gave other such qualifications. Trump won't hear the qualifications, just the praise. And that bodes ill for the future.

APRIL 12, 2017: SPICER FAILS HIS HISTORY TEST

NOT NORMAL: Stating that Hitler did not use chemical weapons.

NOT NORMAL: Clarifying that he didn't use it on his own people.

NOT NORMAL: Referring to Nazi death camps as "Holocaust Centers."

NOT NORMAL: Seeking out Sheldon Adelson to apologize "if he was offended."

NOT NORMAL: Keeping your job after all of this.

---

14 David Frum, "Seven Lessons from Trump's Syria Strike," *The Atlantic*, April 7, 2017, https://www.theatlantic.com/politics/archive/2017/04/seven-lessons-from-trumps-syria-strike/522327/.

Anyone who thinks the omission of the mention of Jews back on Holocaust Remembrance Day was an isolated incident isn't paying attention.

APRIL 14, 2017: TRUMP TRUTHS (AS OPPOSED TO TRUMP LIES, WHICH ARE MUCH MORE PREVALENT)

I was going to write about Syria and Russia again this morning, but as has become usual things are moving so fast (bombing our allies in Syria, dropping a huge bomb in Afghanistan, changing positions on China, NATO, Kushner vs. Bannon, and the list goes on). So instead let's take a step back.

What do we know about Trump (I think most of these are indisputable)?

He knows nothing about policy and doesn't care to learn. He's admitted this (whenever he says, "Who knew?" it means "I didn't know").

He says whatever comes into his head, its relationship to the truth is irrelevant.

He is sexist and fosters racism and anti-Semitism.

He is unduly influenced by whoever he spoke to last or saw on television last.

He sees money as the ultimate arbiter of talent (hence his lust for it, and his respect for those who have it).

All of this means that he is subject to grifters hungry for power. There is no way that Bannon, Manafort, Sessions, and others would get anywhere close to a president who knew anything or understood the responsibility of the position. China has figured this out, give him trademarks that enrich his family, flatter him, and all of a sudden you are no longer a currency manipulator. Putin, who may now have some buyer's remorse, will figure it out too.

In domestic policy this has left his administration quickly adrift. He can't convince Congress of anything because he doesn't know anything and because he won't appoint people who do (and he constantly distracts from any attempt by his underlings to form a consistent message). I'm actually cheered by the lack of accomplishments here.

In foreign policy, however, he doesn't need to convince anyone. He can give orders to the military (or equally alarmingly, let them do what they want). He can make statements that will reverberate around the globe and give faith to dictators (that's why Assad felt comfortable gassing his own people—Trump had said he was fine with Assad). Presidents usually turn to foreign policy after their domestic agendas have stalled (or when circumstances force them to). Never before has that occurred after only three months. And as long as he is in power, it will be hard to curtail his influence here.

APRIL 18, 2017: THE WORST THING HE'S DONE

As we approach one hundred days, there are many contenders. The Muslim ban and the appointment of Sessions are my particular favorites. But something happened yesterday that may be a surprise contender. Trump called Erdogan to congratulate him on the passage of the Turkish constitutional referendum. Why is this bad? Let us count the ways:

1. It is very NOT NORMAL for a US president to call another leader regarding the passage of a referendum in their country.
2. Erdogan has become increasingly autocratic, jailing forty thousand of his opponents since the attempted coup last year.
3. There are credible reports that the election was not free and fair.
4. The referendum will concentrate more power in the hand of President Erdogan, some have described it as "ending Turkish democracy."
5. As I've noted before, this tells autocrats everywhere that Trump has their back. It tells dissidents everywhere that they are on their own.
6. It tells us what Trump would like to see happen in this country. Thank the founders for not allowing the constitution to be amended by referendum!

It takes years to build up credibility. It only takes a moment to lose it. The United States' credibility as a beacon for freedom and democracy has taken a huge hit.

APRIL 20, 2017: GEORGIA ON OUR MINDS

What does Jon Ossoff's winning 48.1 percent of the vote in the GA-6 House race mean? First some data to put it in context.

Hillary Clinton won 47 percent of the vote in November.

If you rank districts by the degree to which they are trending Democratic, GA-6 comes in eighth in the country.

But Tom Price won the seat by twenty points in November.

The bottom line is thus that this is good news but not terribly surprising news. Ossoff and Republican Karen Handel will have a tightly fought race in the runoff for the seat in June. An outright win by Ossoff on Tuesday would have been great. He slightly outperformed the polls but was well within the margin of error. This is the type of district the Democrats want to win but not one they have to win to take the House back in 2018. Taking it in June means Republicans will have to fight an incumbent who will be harder (and costlier) than defending one.

The key is keeping up the level of excitement that this race produced across the country. And not just for House races but just as importantly for state legislative races (this year in New Jersey and Virginia and next year everywhere else). Get informed, spread the word, volunteer, donate, and maybe just maybe run for office. Ossoff is a thirty-year-old, and his audacity in running now seems brilliant.

APRIL 23, 2017: FRANCE ON OUR MINDS

As you probably know, today is the presidential election in France. Geopolitically it is the most important one since ours in November. And it is nuts. There are four candidates who are almost within the margin of error of each other.

Le Pen: The anti-Semitic, racist anti-immigrant. Bannon and Trump supported candidate. Putin likes her too.

Fillon: The scandal-plagued conservative anti-immigrant, anti-Islam candidate. Putin likes him too. But he probably isn't a fascist.

Macron: The former investment banker who supports the EU and does not affiliate with a political party. A centrist but also a bit of a cipher.

Melenchon: The far left (even for France) candidate. Likes Hugo Chavez.

It's not exactly a group to make France proud. If no candidate gets 50 percent, there will be a runoff between the top two. This is certain to happen. That means among these four candidates, there are six possible outcomes (four choose two for probability nerds). My objective function places a lot of value on Le Pen losing. Second most important would be Macron winning. Therefore, I'd rank the six possible runoffs thusly:

1. Macron-Melenchon: Macron almost certainly becomes President. Le Pen certainly does not.
2. Macron-Fillon: Toss up in the general election. Le Pen out.
3. Fillon-Melenchon: Here we get to the not so good ones. Fillon probably wins. Le Pen out.
4. Macron-Le Pen: Macron probably wins, but Le Pen not out.
5. Le Pen-Fillon: Fillon probably wins, and Le Pen not out.
6. Le Pen-Melenchon: Who knows who wins? Who knows what happens to Europe?

APRIL 26, 2017: THE FIRST NINETY-SEVEN DAYS

I've never felt constrained by the oppressive norm of base ten, so let's take stock (consolidating a few themes that have run through my posts):

NORMAL (or indications that Trump is a typical Republican president).

Appointed and won confirmation of a very conservative Supreme Court justice.

Signed a dozen statutes repealing late Obama era regulations (it hasn't been done before, but any Republican president would have done the same).

Delayed numerous other regulations and signed executive orders to begin exploring the repeal of others (this may never come to anything but it may).

Increase military activity around the globe (but the degree of discretion given the military is NOT NORMAL).

Increase immigration enforcement (but the degree of discretion given to ICE agents is NOT NORMAL).

NOT NORMAL (indications that Trump is incompetent, and we are in for four years of chaos).

Insulted Australia, Canada, Germany, and many other allies.

Appointed Betsy DeVos, Ben Carson, and Rex Tillerson to cabinet who combine for zero days of relevant experience to their jobs.

Failed to advance even one piece of significant legislation in a Congress controlled by his party.

NOT NORMAL (indications that Trump is a budding authoritarian).

Complimented Erdogan, and refused to say bad things about Putin.

Appointed racists, Jeff Sessions and Stephen Bannon, to powerful positions.

Used the presidency to profit himself and his family (too many instances to mention).

Remained under suspicion for his campaign conspiring with Russia to win the election (make no mistake, Russia conspired—just no evidence yet that Trump or his campaign did).

Tweeted repeatedly; gave interviews that sounded more like your angry grandfather than the leader of the free world. Alleged that his predecessor wiretapped him, that many of those who voted against him did so illegally, exaggerated the crowd size at his inauguration, and (hot off the presses) that judges were endangering lives by ruling against him.

It has been a very NOT NORMAL ninety-seven days. And he's not going to change. So let's hope the next ninety-seven show progress on getting rid of him.

APRIL 30, 2017: BACK TO (NOT) NORMAL

On Friday David Brooks wrote that Trump was becoming more normal. After three or four days with little for me to write about, I was wondering if Brooks might be right. Then in twenty-four hours:

- Trump described the legislative process as archaic when explaining why he hadn't gotten more done in his first one hundred days.

- Trump held a rally in Harrisburg, Pennsylvania, that was a campaign rally for a sitting president where the attendees chanted "Lock Her Up," and Trump savaged the media.
- Trump invited Philippine President Rodrigo Duterte to the White House. Duterte has actively encouraged vigilantism in his country and may have even killed people himself.

He's not changing. He's not gonna change. He wasn't qualified to be president when he won the primary. He wasn't qualified when he won the election. He's not qualified today. And he would much rather be dictator than president. I linked to a column yesterday about not getting complacent just because we have stifled Trump in his first one hundred days. As if on cue, Trump reminded us why there is still a lot of hard work ahead.

MAY 2, 2017: TRUMP PRAISES JACKSON

Normal versus Not Normal, 1830s edition.

NORMAL (sadly): Enacting measures leading to the deaths of Native Americans.

NOT NORMAL: Destroying the Bank of the United States and paving the way for numerous nineteenth-century recessions.

NORMAL: Threatening to send the navy to South Carolina when it threatens secession over a tariff.

NOT NORMAL: Being able to stop a Civil War sixteen years after you're dead.

(As for modern times: Thinking that Jackson, a slaveholder, would have "solved" the cause of the Civil War is NOT NORMAL. He would have either invaded the south to stop secession or never done anything to threaten slavery. As one historian on Twitter said, "Jackson would have hung the secessionists and the abolitionists—that would have been his solution [and perhaps Trump's])."

MAY 5, 2017: OBAMACARE REPEAL PASSES THE HOUSE

Angry!

I'm angry this morning.

I'm angry that 219 representatives of the people feel sufficiently comfortable in their electoral safety that they voted for a bill that strips health insurance from millions and helps no one but the very wealthy.

I'm angry that these 219 representatives may have felt that the Senate will save their asses by either killing the bill or stripping out the worst provisions. Such cynical behavior and a willingness to gamble with the lives of millions are unfitting of a representative of the people.

I'm angry that regardless of what happens in the Senate, the chance that millions will lose health insurance is significantly greater today than it was yesterday.

I'm angry that a group of old white men (and I'm already two out of three in that category and rapidly approaching the third) can chortle over a beer after passing what one person described as one of the most regressive bills in American history.

I'm angry enough that I gave my first donation of the 2018 cycle yesterday. I've been urging people to call their representatives in Washington. Now when you call, you should threaten them with giving to their opponents if they don't vote the way you want. And you know what, you don't have to live in their districts to make this a threat that is relevant to them.

MAY 8, 2017: DON'T FORGET ABOUT RUSSIA (WOW! THIS ONE WAS TIMELY)

As the French show us that you don't always have to pay attention to e-mails leaked by a foreign power, it's a good time to check in on the least NORMAL aspect of this administration: the possibility that they collaborated with that foreign power to win the 2016 election.

It's been a quiet several weeks. That may change with the testimony today of former acting Attorney General Sally Yates before Congress. Despite the quiet before today, the investigation is likely churning along. And despite whatever excitement occurs today, it is likely that it will still be a while before anything truly significant becomes public. But make no mistake, eventually the investigation is likely to ensnare the four horsemen of the Trump-Russia connection that we know about: Manafort, Stone, Flynn, and Paige. Whether it goes higher who knows?

MAY 9, 2017: TRUMP FIRES COMEY

It's Trump or democracy.

Initial thoughts about the Comey firing…

Let's reason this out.

1. This is not about Comey's handling of the Hillary investigation. There is no reason that Trump would have waited until now if that were the case.
2. The *Times* is reporting that Trump asked Sessions last week to find a reason to fire Comey. Comey testified in public last week and was scheduled to testify in a hearing on Thursday.
3. Trump and those around him know that the optics of firing someone who is investigating you are awful. You wouldn't do it unless you are very scared about something coming out.

The only reasonable conclusion is that Comey was fired because he has learned something or was close to learning something.

So what next…

The Saturday Night Massacre did not help Nixon. It furthered the resolve of his opponents and convinced them that the president had something to hide. But his opponents controlled both Houses of Congress.

Today Trump's opponents control the mainstream press (yeah, it's the one thing he is right about) and numerous statehouses. Whether that is enough to bring him down is an open question. Some in the GOP have to stand up, and the initial indications are not good (Lindsey Graham and Chuck Grassley issued statements supporting Comey's dismissal). But things can change quickly if there is a public outcry.

Back when I did my scenarios, I had the three most likely as a slow impeachment, a quick one, and tyranny. I've waffled a bit about that since then, but today returns me to thinking that if Trump is not removed from office, then democracy in the United States is in trouble. Trump's firing of Comey tells us that there is reason to believe that Trump is guilty of something huge. What it doesn't tell us is if the political will is there to make him pay for it. The weeks ahead will tell us that.

More when I've had more time to think about it.

MAY 10, 2017: READING THE TEA LEAVES

So much going on regarding the Comey firing that I don't have a coherent narrative, just random thoughts.

- We have been reduced to reading our administration much as we used to read the Kremlin (and I assume this was also true for Nixon's time). There is no reason to trust anything they say.
- As one friend pointed out on my previous thread, one can interpret their actions as impulsive and incompetent or malicious. Given that Trump asked for a reason to fire Comey a week ago, the firing came a day after Comey asked for more money to pursue the Russia investigation, and according to CNN, soon after subpoenas were granted by a grand jury investigating l'Affaire Flynn, I lean toward maliciousness. But don't rule out impulsivity. Trump was reportedly yelling at the television whenever Russia came up.
- Remember impeachment is a political decision, not a legal one. Legal findings can influence the politics greatly but in the end, Trump's approval ratings are your best guide to figuring out if impeachment is on the table. As they are currently around forty-one, it is not.
- Reactions from Republican senators are all over the place. McConnell and Cornyn (the leaders) are toeing the Trump line. Others like Graham, Lankford, and Corker have noted Trump's right to fire Comey but questioned the timing. Sasse and Flake have issued the strongest statements. McCain has both waffled and issued the strongest statement in defense of Comey. My guess is that the ten to fifteen sane Republicans in the Senate are struggling mightily right now. They are worried but also know there is huge pressure to defend the president and enact their agenda. Watch them the closest in the weeks ahead. And watch what they do, which often does not measure up to what they say.
- On the doing front though, most interesting (perhaps because it hits the regulatory world I work in) is that the Senate voted down

a resolution that would have overturned curbs on methane emissions 51–49. McCain provided the key vote. This was only the second time McCain had voted against a Trump-supported measure or nomination. Either McCain cares suddenly about climate change or he is sending a signal to McConnell and Trump. In either case, a victory for the environment.

- I am getting no work done today.

MAY 11, 2017: RUMORS AND NOT RUMORS

I don't know that I have seen a day like today in terms of rumors circulating about Trump, the FBI, Comey, and so on, since Election Day. Here are a few things that are not rumors.

- Trump, after letting Huckabee-Sanders and Pence argue that he fired Comey on the advice of Deputy AG Rosenstein, told NBC that he was going to fire him regardless of what the Rosenstein memo said.
- The Senate Intelligence Committee asked the bureau within the Treasury Department that investigates financial crimes for records regarding the dealings of Trump and his associates with Russia.
- The Senate Intelligence Committee also issued its first subpoena. It was to Michael Flynn demanding all records regarding his dealings with Russia.
- Acting FBI Director Andrew McCabe testified before the Senate saying that the Russia investigation would proceed despite Comey's firing. He said other interesting things as well.[15]
- Rosenstein met behind closed doors with the chair and minority leader of the Senate Intelligence Committee.

---

15 Quinta Jurecic, "Takeaways from Acting FBI Director Andrew McCabe's Testimony Today," *Lawfare*, May 11, 2017, https://lawfareblog.com/takeaways-acting-fbi-director-andrew-mccabes-testimony-today

- Deputy Press Secretary Huckabee Sanders said that the Russia investigation should end; then she reversed herself. Then she reversed herself again.

There is plenty of other salacious stuff out there. Hopefully most of it is true. Probably most of it is not.

MAY 15, 2017: APPROVAL RATINGS

Yesterday someone cited the fact that 58 percent of Republicans approve of Jim Comey's dismissal as evidence that Trump is untouchable (8 percent disapprove and 33 percent have no opinion).

Not quite.

August 2–5, 1974, *days* before Nixon quits. Should he resign? Among Republicans: 31 percent YES, 59 percent NO, 10 percent DK.

Now there are differences of course. Much more needs to happen before we reach August 1974. Polarization is much higher now than it was under Nixon.

But when Trump starts to get down into the sixties or low seventies for approval among Republicans, he is in trouble. Last week was a step in that direction. Let's see what this week brings.

MAY 16, 2017: THE NEW NEWS CYCLE

1. Trump does something outrageous.
2. Staff denies it.
3. Conservative media denies it blames liberals for leaking it.
4. Liberal elite writes thoughtful pieces about it and how what Trump did was unprecedented, cataclysmic, the beginning of the end for him.
5. Trump admits it and brags about it.
6. Republican senators express concern. One says something mildly encouraging.
7. I post on Facebook about it.

8. The more conspiracy minded insist that indictments are right around the corner, and this blunder is a sign.
9. The country is weakened a bit more.
10. Go to step 1.

MAY 17, 2017: THE REPUBLICAN CHOICE

Probably the question I've seen most often this past week is "What will it take for congressional Republicans to turn on Trump?" The answer may be the cumulative events of the past week (Comey firing, Trump giving classified intelligence to the Russians, and yesterday, the Comey memo). But it may also take a bit longer (I feel better than I have that it's coming though). Why?

1. The tax-cut explanation. This one is a favorite of those of us on the left. Republicans are so giddy about the possibility of tax cuts and repealing Obamacare, that they are willing to put up with a little treason to get it. I don't dismiss this out of hand, but I think achieving the policy goals of the GOP is a side benefit of keeping Trump.

2. The conspiracy theory. If (as I have done a bit in the past two months) you follow the conspiracy left, you see the theory that whatever Trump is guilty of will bring down Pence and Ryan as well. Stories about money laundering, Russian influence, and an international conspiracy abound. This would explain the hesitation to go after Trump: too many powerful people would fall, and the party would be ruined. I don't buy this either, but I have gone from upgrading its likelihood from 0.1 percent to about 1 percent.

3. The voters. Aha! People, it is always the voters. Republicans in the House generally live in pretty safe districts (mostly due to voter clustering, but also gerrymandering). Therefore, they have to worry about primaries more than general elections. And who can you bet will vote in primaries? Trump supporters! Even if Trump does drop to the Nixonian level of 60 percent support within the Republican Party, many of those 60 percent are likely to vote

and remember who betrayed their racist orange-haired leader. Politicians are a nervous lot. Threats to their reelection are always foremost in their mind.

This is why, even with yesterday's news, there may still need to be some more revelations left before the House turns on Trump and begins to consider impeachment. It is also why the Twenty-fifth Amendment (which has never been used, and I'm not sure anyone knows how it would work) may be a more pleasant alternative for Republicans than impeachment. But if there are more memos or tapes out there, and the one described yesterday is the tip of the iceberg (as I hope and suspect it might be), then Trump's support may drop low enough that even House Republicans will have to think about bailing on him.

Keep in mind though that a president has never been impeached by a Congress controlled by his own party. A NOT NORMAL way to end a NOT NORMAL presidency?

MAY 18, 2017: MUELLER GETS APPOINTED

I'm already wondering what I am going to miss when I am offline between five and six this evening. Yesterday's news was the appointment of a Special Counsel by Deputy Attorney General Ron Rosenstein (putting Rosenstein in line for the coveted "Comeback of the Week" award).

As the 538 piece below points out, this actually helps Republicans in Congress in the short run (possibly) by taking some of the pressure off them. Now they can answer all Trump-related questions by saying, "Let's wait and see what Mueller finds out." However, we should keep the pressure on Congress to move forward with its own investigations for two reasons (based on my imperfect understanding of special counsels):

- The Special Counsel is investigating crimes. There may be many things that are not necessarily prosecutable that the public should know about. What if the Trump campaign was not quite guilty of collusion with Russia but still gave Putin winks and nods. We should know that a congressional investigation will bring that out.

- The Special Counsel is not obligated to tell the public everything he finds. Sure, Mueller will have to disclose information on anyone he decides to prosecute, but he does not have to do so for those for whom he feels there is insufficient evidence to pursue. A congressional investigation (or one by a congressionally appointed commission) would be public. And it would impose political costs on the Trump administration.

MAY 20, 2017: STUPID, SUICIDAL, OR SAFE?

The news yesterday that Trump actually bragged to the *Russians* that he had fired Comey in order to cut off the investigation into his connections with *Russia* struck me as the most bizarre twist yet. Up until now, you could say that the unraveling of the Trump administration over the past few weeks was like a movie. Yesterday's addition was an element that even the trashiest of movie producers would have discarded as too unrealistic.

Why would he do that? The simplest (and in my mind most likely) explanation is that Trump is really as stupid as his biggest critics think. After all the leaks he has had, could he really think that saying the sentence out loud that would most directly implicate him would remain private? Only an idiot would do that, right? You could argue that he is just very impulsive, but this is a degree of impulsiveness that I would call stupid.

Or does he really want this all to end? He's clearly miserable being president. His actions over the past week or two, starting with the firing of Comey, have been so relentlessly self-destructive that maybe he wants to be impeached. Then (assuming he's not in a jail cell) he can go out have his rallies, talk about how he was railroaded, and do what he enjoys.

Or maybe he knows (or thinks he knows) that he really could shoot a man on Fifth Avenue and be safe. His supporters will never leave him and that will keep enough Republicans in Congress in line that impeachment hearings are a pipe dream of the left.

So I ask again, stupid, suicidal, or safe?

MAY 22, 2017: TIME FOR NORMAL VERSUS NOT NORMAL, SAUDI ARABIA EDITION

(remember, NORMAL does not necessarily mean good):

NORMAL: Kissing up to the Saudi royalty (just ask the Bush family).

NORMAL: Selling weapons to the Saudis (although Obama halted some arms sales for a while).

NORMAL: Using harsh rhetoric to describe Iran (which indeed deserves much of it).

NOT NORMAL: Kissing up to the Saudi royalty after insulting Saudi Arabia and Islam throughout your campaign. Selling weapons to Saudi Arabia when you know the country will now use them in Yemen to attack Iranian-based forces, which is an action you have just basically encouraged with your anti-Iran speech. Giving this speech two days after Iran reelects a moderate president (for them) in an election in which women are allowed to vote, something that appears to be eons away from happening in Saudi Arabia.

Context matters.

NOT NORMAL Your daughter's charity accepting a $100 million donation from the Saudis the day after the speech when you recently criticized the foundation run by Bill Clinton for accepting a similar $10–25 million donation after Hilary left office.

Also NOT NORMAL, this picture.

MAY 23, 2017: THE POLITICS OF IMPEACHMENT

Nate Silver does a great analysis[16] of what it would take to impeach Trump. The bottom line: if Congress decides it wants to impeach Trump, there is probably already enough of a cause to do so. The key step is the Republican-controlled Congress wanting to do so.

I've said for a while that those of us hoping to be rid of Trump need to watch political indicators more than legal ones. It was nice to see yesterday that Flynn took the fifth, and Stone and Manafort turned over documents. But neither of those will move the political needle much. The legal news needs to be big to have a political impact though. Perhaps the news about Trump asking Coats and Rogers to deny collusion between the Trump campaign and Russia will add to last week's really big revelations. Unfortunately that seems to have been upstaged by the awfulness in Manchester.

But if you want good political signs, here are two.

1. Reports show a tightening race in Thursday's special election to replace Ryan Zinke as the representative in Congress from Montana. According to one report, of the seats currently held by Republicans, this one is the 120th most likely to flip. If the Democrats win it or even come within five points, then House Republicans will and should be worried. Meanwhile Jon Ossoff, the Democrat running for Congress in Georgia to replace Tom Price, had some good news yesterday. A new poll showed him winning by seven points. It's only one poll, and the election isn't until next month, but a win there would also be a loud shot across Trump's bow.

2. *Fox News* fell to third in the cable news ratings for the first time in seventeen years. To those worried that the conservative bubble is unbreakable, this is a great sign. Fewer people watching *Fox* will eventually translate into fewer people supporting Trump.

---

16 Nate Silver, "Will Donald Trump be Impeached," *FiveThirtyEight*, May 22, 2017, https://fivethirtyeight.com/features/chance-donald-trump-impeached/.

MAY 25, 2017: PLAYING WITH (REALLY BIG) NUMBERS

In late April, the Trump administration released its one-page, vaguely described tax-cut plan. And on Tuesday, it released its proposed budget.

It's no surprise that the numbers don't add up.

First, the budget: if you add up the numbers the way most people who learn addition would do, it will increase the deficit by $2.3 trillion. But when the Trump administration adds up the numbers, it does no such thing. How is this possible?

Only by tax-cut magic! First, the administration assumes that the tax cut will generate economic growth, to the extent that it will not only pay for itself but also lead to increased revenues to cover the increased deficit. Supply side economics at its finest. You won't find a credible economist to support this argument.

But this isn't even the administration's worst abuse of the numbers. Not only will the tax cut create mythical growth-related revenue but it also will have no countervailing negative impact. That's right: the Trump budget's estimates simply ignore the uncontroversial fact that when you cut taxes, you bring in less money. The tax cut could *reduce* revenue by as much as $5 trillion.

So for those of you adding at home, there is a hole of $7.3 trillion in the Trump budget estimates. Let's put error bars on that and say the deficit will increase by between $6 and $8 trillion.

Why does it matter? In addition to the bad macroeconomic effects of such high deficits, the Trump budget also cuts hundreds of programs that help the least fortunate in the name of fiscal responsibility. If the Trump administration really cared about fiscal responsibility, it wouldn't propose a tax cut of $5 trillion and pretend that this will actually increase the amount of money coming into the government. If the Republicans in Congress who have pretended to care about fiscal responsibility actually care, then they will kill the tax cut first and then work on a budget.

In reality, they will likely cut taxes and then pass a budget that cuts some of the programs Trump wants to cut (Medicaid may be in particular danger) but not many of them. Deficits will skyrocket, and then they will say we need to cut more programs for the poor because of...fiscal responsibility.

MAY 26, 2017: WHAT MONTANA MEANS

Yesterday Republican and aspiring brownshirt Greg Gianforte won the open congressional seat in Montana by about seven points. What does it mean? Here is some context.

Donald Trump won Montana (the entire state is a congressional district) by twenty points.

Ryan Zinke (running as a Republican incumbent) won the seat by fifteen points in November.

With Trump's declining approval ratings and an open seat, an improvement on the fifteen- to twenty-point range was expected. The amount of the improvement is also about what the best political analysts expected and indicates a good environment for Democrats nationally.

Moral victories grow tiresome in the absence of real victories. But if you do want to feel good this morning, know that there are approximately 120 districts held by Republicans that are more favorable than (MT-AL). That means there are 120 GOP members of Congress not sleeping well these days. The Dems only have to unseat twenty-four of them (and protect their own seats) to win a majority.

Finally, though, there is the body-slamming of the reporter by Gianforte on the eve of the election. While I know logically that the result is positive, and two-thirds of people in Montana voted before the incident, I find it impossible not to be depressed by it. The attacks on the press come from Trump's rhetoric, and they are indicative of a desire for suppression of the free press. The tepid reaction by Republicans to the incident was appalling. Eliminating a free press is always the first step on the way to authoritarianism. This would be a better country if Gianforte was heading to prison instead of to Congress.

MAY 26, 2017: THE "RAINBOW TOUR"

As Trump returns from his first trip abroad, I am reminded of the song from Evita, "Rainbow Tour." With apologies to Andrew Lloyd Weber, here are some adapted lyrics:

[Bannon:]
People of the world, I send you the Trump of America

[Hillary]
The Saudis have fallen to the charms of Donald
He can do what he likes, it doesn't matter much
[Aide #1:]
He's our man of the new world with a golden touch
[Aide #2:]
He got a Golden medal and touched the orb
[Hillary]
But if you're not President Obama, that's not hard

[Aide #1:]
The King's reign in Arabia should see out the decade
So you've just acquired an ally who
Looks as secure in his job as you
[Aide #2:]
But more important current political thought is
Your hatred of Iran a phenomenal asset, your trump card

[Chorus:]

[Bannon and Aides:]
Let's hear it for the Rainbow Tour
It's been an incredible success
We weren't quite sure, we had a few doubts

[Bannon:] Would Trump win through?
[Aides:] But the answer is yes

[Bannon:]
There you are, I told you so
Makes no difference where he goes
The whole world over just the same
Just listen to them call his name
And who would underestimate the tycoon now?

[Hillary]
Now I don't like to spoil a wonderful story
But the news from Israel isn't quite as good
He hasn't gone down like they thought he would
Israel unconvinced by Trump's glory
They think he gave up their intelligence, can't think why

[Aide #2:]
More bad news from Rome; he met with the Pope
He only got a lecture on climate change, a kindly word
[Hillary]
I wouldn't say the Holy Father gave him the bird
But papal decorations, never a hope

[chorus]

[Bannon:] Will Trump win through?
[Aides:] But the answer is...
[Hillary] A qualified
[Aides:] Yes

[Hillary]
Trump started badly no question, in Brussels
Pushing the head of Montenegro out of his way
An ugly reminder of the Brexit day
He could have won friends, he had the chance
But he suddenly seemed to lose interest
He looked tired

[Hillary]
Face the facts, the Rainbow's starting to fade
I don't think he'll make it to England now

[Aide #1:]
It wasn't on the schedule anyhow

[Hillary]
You'd better get out the flags and fix a parade
Some kind of coming home in triumph is required

[chorus]

[Aide #2:] Would Trump win through?
[Aide #1:] And the answer is
[Aide #2:] Yes
[Hillary] And no
[Aides:] And yes
[Hillary] And no
[Aides:] And yes
[Hillary] No

MAY 29, 2017: THE RACE

Around Inauguration Day, I outlined four scenarios (I later added a fifth) for the Trump administration:

1. A slow march toward impeachment or resignation
2. A polarizing event that leads to impeachment or resignation
3. Authoritarianism
4. A typical Republican presidency
5. Chaos and the slow erosion of America's place in the world

I bounced back and forth between scenarios 1, 3, and 5 as most likely. I still think 5 is quite possible, but the past few weeks have put me (again) in the camp that we are most likely in a race between the end of Trump's presidency and authoritarianism.

Impeachment pulled ahead over the past three weeks. The firing of Comey unleashed a series of reverberations that have damaged Trump. His approval ratings have dropped to 38 percent, and he may be on the verge of losing one or more of his key advisers. If his approval drops to the low thirties, impeachment will be in play. Finally, he showed yesterday that he still loves tweeting (clearly he was told Twitter was unavailable in Europe and the Middle East), which can only hurt him.

But Trump-Bannon will not go quietly, and make no mistake about it, their goal is still the erosion of democracy (in Bannon's case this is a conscious goal; in Trump's I'm less sure). The worst sign of the past few weeks has been the rallying around Trump by his military appointments, particularly McMaster and DHS Secretary Kelly. Many had hoped that these generals would act as a brake on his worst tendencies. But McMaster defended the Jared Kushner back channel to the Russians, and Kelly has been right there with Trump on many issues. An attack on North Korea or a terrorist attack here will only serve to bind the military more closely to Trump.

The other bad sign is that Republicans that one might think are sane like Graham and Corker continue to be unwilling to move beyond "expressing concern" about Trump and even defend him on some occasions. With GOP leaders still willing to defend him, Trump can continue to attack the press and erode democratic norms with impunity. I still think that will change if Trump's approval drops low enough.

The clock is ticking. Even as Trump is without policy victories, he continues to run roughshod over these norms. I started this administration with the feeling that either Trump's presidency or American democracy will not survive until 2020. That feeling continues to linger.

MAY 30, 2017: IMAGINING THE WORST

The past four months have been nuts. We haven't gone more than a few days without seeing a revelation that would have shocked us a year ago. And yet…we see article after article about 2018 or 2020, about the prospects for legislation in Congress, and about the inner dynamics of the

Trump administration. Articles that would not seem out of place in 2010 or 2005.

As the Eric Garland tweetstorm I shared on Sunday (again in comments) points out though, this helps us forget that we are in NOT NORMAL times. The president has used the office to enrich himself. His election was aided by a foreign power that has an interest in destabilizing us. His campaign (and maybe he) may have collaborated with this foreign power. He has likely acted to obstruct the investigation of this collaboration and his financial ties to Russia. NOT NORMAL. NOT NORMAL, NOT NORMAL.

So when looking to the future, we (and journalists in particular) need to admit to ourselves that what was once unthinkable is now possible. Do I think the Trump administration will bomb North Korea in order to enhance his political prospects? No. But is it plausible? Yes. Has the probability of this gone up in the past few weeks? Also yes. Do I think that such an act or a terrorist attack will be used as a pretext to jail journalists? No. But is it plausible? Yes. Has the probability of this gone up in the past few weeks? Also yes. Do I think that internment camps of Muslims will happen? No. But is it plausible? Yes. Has the probability of this gone up in the past few weeks? Also yes.

Daniel Kahneman and others have written about "optimism bias." One aspect of optimism bias is the tendency to minimize risks. It is one of the ways we cope with unpleasant possibilities. Sometimes it is healthy; it helps us soldier on in the face of daunting odds. Sometimes it is dangerous; it leads us to ignore things that we can prevent. Other research has indicated that we are bad at understanding probabilities, particularly small ones. We are not well equipped to understand the importance of something moving from a one-in-a-thousand risk to a one-in-a-hundred risk. And some of the adverse events above may have moved into the one in a hundred range (or more). That's a big deal. And a reason to remember that nothing is NORMAL.

I don't mean to harp on the scary scenarios to bring everyone down. But if we don't view these scenarios as possibilities, if we buy into the narrative that most things are NORMAL, we are less prepared to fight the steps leading up to the worst scenarios. The decline of democracy in the United States is still unlikely. But the least likely part of it was the election of someone like Donald Trump. And that happened.

JUNE 1, 2017: THE POLITICS AND POLICY OF PUNTING PARIS

(or how to look at the glass as 1/10 full rather than 9/10 empty)

As you know by now, Trump will be pulling us out of the Paris climate accord today. Obviously this is a brazen insult to the rest of the world. How much will it affect the climate though?

The key is remembering the baseline. Even if he hadn't bailed on Paris, Trump would still be president. The key from the perspective of saving the planet is not so much being a part of the accord, as what we would do to reach the emission reduction targets associated with it. And a Trump administration was not going to do much. Regardless of whether he stayed in the accord, he was gonna try and undo the Clean Power Plan, the mileage standards, and anything else President Obama did to reduce the carbon emissions that lead to climate change.

And if he had stayed in the accord and reversed President Obama's initiatives, it would have signaled to other signatories that not meeting your goal is an option. It would have rendered the treaty meaningless. Now, signatories know they will have to leave the treaty if they want to renege.

OK, enough positive spin. This decision is still a disaster even if it has no long-term impact on the climate. Coupled with Trump's actions in Europe last week, he further erodes our position of influence in the world on all issues, further signals to global bad actors that they can cite the United States as an example, and further strengthens China's hand both diplomatically and as a worldwide economic leader in renewable energy. All of these are unambiguously bad for us and for many of the world's people.

I'd like to say that this will hurt Trump domestically, but I'm not sure it will. While a majority now believe that climate change is man-made, my guess is that the vast majority of his supporters do not. And since it's all about driving his approval down to possible impeachment levels, we don't even get that out of this debacle.

JUNE 3, 2017: RUSSIA, RUSSIA, RUSSIA

It has been a comparatively quiet week on the Trump-Russia front. But don't worry, with the testimony next week of James Comey, things will pick up again quickly.

Still, I hear too often that the Russia investigation is a distraction from the real damage that is being done by Trump's presidency. I think that is dead wrong for two reasons.

First, on its own merits, the possibility (actually in my view, the likelihood) that Russia successfully influenced the outcome of our election is terrifying. When you add in that Trump is possibly (again in my view probably) trying to cover up his campaign's connections to Russia, it becomes the biggest scandal in American history. Finally, the possibility of an alliance of nuclear-armed autocrats who believe in white Christian supremacy redefines "worst possible outcome." It would make all that real damage permanent.

But let's say you don't buy the Russian influence or you doubt its importance. To you I say, it's the only game in town for going after Trump. A Trump presidency that lasts for four years will be a cataclysm in all of the policy areas you care about. It's the Russia scandal that is slowing down his progress right now in the executive branch and in the legislative branch. It's the Russia scandal that is the only path to impeachment (maybe emoluments but much less likely). And it's the Russia scandal that has produced the most self-destructive tweets from the covfefe in chief.

Remember Al Capone didn't go to jail for the St. Valentine's Day massacre, it was tax evasion. Richard Nixon wasn't forced to resign for bombing Cambodia but for covering up a "third-rate burglary." I think this is much, much bigger, but you don't have to.

If you worry that health care will be taken away from the most vulnerable, care about Russia. If you care about the enabling of discriminatory policing that is going on at DOJ, then care about Russia. If you care about the deportation of individuals who have spent years in this country, then care about Russia. If you care about the climate, then care about Russia. Don't stop caring about the issues that make you passionate, but also care about Russia.

JUNE 5, 2017: THE TWEETER IN CHIEF

In the past seventy-two hours, our president did the following on Twitter:

- Attacked the mayor of London repeatedly after the terror attacks there. Think about this as if Tony Blair had attacked Rudy Giuliani after 9/11 (not my analogy, but a great one). He's done this despite British Prime Minister Theresa May defending Mayor Khan. There goes another ally.
- Undermined the defense of his executive order by calling it a "travel ban" despite repeated arguments by his lawyers that it was no such thing. He did this multiple times.
- Insulted his own Department of Justice for watering down the travel ban. This one bears quoting: "The Justice Dept. should ask for an expedited hearing of the watered down Travel Ban before the Supreme Court - & seek much tougher version!" Who does he think the Justice Department reports to?
- Used the London attack to talk about gun control, ignoring the fact that if guns were easier to get in England, the number of fatalities would have been much greater.
- Complained about the lack of confirmations of his appointees, while at the same time lagging behind previous administrations on nominating people (in part because he is having trouble getting people to work for him).

Even for Trump, this is an amazing set of tweets in a short period of time. You don't need me to tell you that this is NOT NORMAL. The question is, is it?

a) Trump reacting to news reports (some of the Tweets were clearly in response to Joe Scarborough and *Fox and Friends*) and regaining access to his Twitter account (i.e., NORMAL for Trump).
b) Trump losing his mind even further.
c) Trump stressed about the Comey testimony later this week and the gathering pressure on him and his aides (and family).

Your call (multiple answers are acceptable).

JUNE 7, 2017: RUNNING OUT OF WORDS

The *New York Times* ran an article last night (and in today's print edition) with the title "Comey Told Sessions: Don't Leave Me Alone With Trump."

I just don't know what to say. I started NORMAL versus NOT NORMAL to (a) give people an idea about how much Trump was doing that violated American norms, (b) point out those actions that were getting a lot of criticism but were standard for Republican presidents, and (c) help to put a brake on the normalization of Trump as president. But with a headline like this, we have left NORMAL so far behind that I'm not sure that we will ever see NORMAL again as long as Trump is president.

Just yesterday, in addition to this story:

- Trump bragged on Twitter about creating a crisis in the Middle East that has experts on the area very worried (the Saudi blockade of Qatar). Oh, and we have a military base in Qatar.
- Dan Coats, the Director of National Intelligence, says that he was asked by Trump to interfere with Comey's investigation.
- A pro-Trump group announced that it was going to be airing ads calling Comey a "political showboat" during Comey's testimony.
- Rumors circulated that Trump will be live-tweeting Comey's testimony.

Do we need another category beyond NOT NORMAL? Really, really Not Normal? Surreal?

JUNE 9, 2017: LOOKING AHEAD AFTER COMEY

So here are my three big takeaways from yesterday:

1. Comey said the president lied and basically said Trump is being investigated for obstruction of justice by Mueller.
2. The Republicans are still very much on board with defending Trump.
3. Despite the above, don't ignore the fact that we had a hearing on the behavior of a Republican president in a Republican Senate five months into the president's tenure. This doesn't happen, if Trump isn't in some trouble.

So what now? There are two major milestones coming up in the next month (not counting the unexpected Trump-generated crises and Trump tweets). And both involve something you can do.

1. The special election in GA-6. Democrat Jon Ossoff is up by a tiny amount in the race to replace Tom Price. This is a Republican district, but there is a real shot at an actual victory rather than just a symbolic one like the ones Democrats won in Kansas and Montana. You can give money or make calls.
2. Even bigger, the Senate is trying to rush through its own replacement for Obamacare. The Senate calendar is such that if they don't get it passed (passage won't make it law; it will still need to be reconciled with the House bill) by the July 4 recess, it will be very hard for them to pass a final bill this year. And if they don't pass it this year, then it is unlikely they will take it up in an election year. Call your senator and tell him or her to oppose the health-care bill. Call Dean Heller (R-NV) and Jeff Flake (R-AZ) and tell them you'll donate to their opponents in 2018 if they vote for the bill.

This is big both for its own sake (the repeal is likely to be marginally better than the House bill but still awful) but also because one of the reasons for Senators to look the other way on Trump is because turning on him would create such a ruckus that passing legislation will be very hard. If they realize, they aren't even getting legislation passed, then their incentive to turn on Trump increases. It all fits together.

JUNE 12, 2017: COINCIDENCE OR CONSPIRACY

I've spent much of my life deriding conspiracy theories. I don't think Big Pharma suppresses studies on autism-vaccine linkages. I don't think Bush knew about 9/11 in advance. When my preferred candidate loses, I don't assume there was cheating on the other side.

Any social scientist worth their salt has the idea that correlation does not imply causation. Reading behavioral economics, one reads a lot about the brain's desire to see patterns where none exist. Coincidence and randomness are often better explanations than causality.

So why have I bought into the Trump Russia conspiracy? Well, I haven't bought into all of it. But the idea that Trump or high-level aides illegally conspired with Russia to lift sanctions before taking office and may have known about the DNC hack both strike me as plausible. The number of indicators of something being wrong is just too high. We know all of the following with a high level of confidence.

1. Trump is indebted to Russian banks.
2. There are myriad connections between Russia and his top staff.
3. Trump got the anti-Russia provision struck from the Republican platform.
4. Russia hacked the DNC and leaked the e-mails to Wikileaks (Note: I think that Putin, like many of us, thought HRC would win; he was just trying to weaken her presidency and now may have buyer's remorse).
5. Roger Stone, Trump confidante, predicted the leaks a few days before they came out.
6. Flynn discussed sanction relief with the Russians before the inauguration.
7. Trump continually praises Putin.
8. Sessions had undisclosed meetings with Russians.

9. Kushner asked for a back-channel way to communicate with the Russians out of the ears of intelligence.
10. Trump asked Comey to go easy on Flynn.
11. Trump fired Comey.

Now one can come up with alternative stories to explain some of these. Trump likes authoritarians, so he praises Putin. Trump is self-conscious about his electoral loss, so he wants to discredit the Russia hacking story. I even think some of these alternative stories are true. But there are two problems with relying on the alternative theories.

a. You need a bunch of them to explain the pattern above.
b. Even some of the alternatives point at potentially criminal behavior (if Trump fired Comey to get off Flynn, it doesn't really matter if Russia is at the heart of the matter or not—it's still a problem).

Now there are conspiracy theorists who go too far (Louise Mensch, for example), but we are getting to the point where there is an awful lot of smoke for there not to be a fire.

JUNE 13, 2017: TRUMP ASKS HIS CABINET FOR PRAISE

Yesterday's "Let's go around the table and say something nice about me" cabinet meeting was NORMAL…for North Korea. For the United States it was arguable the least normal thing that has happened yet.

JUNE 14, 2017: TRUMP SPEAKS THE TRUTH

Yup, it's a classic man bites dog story. Yesterday Trump called the health-care bill passed by the GOP last month "mean." Ha! He's right. He made the comment in a meeting with a dozen GOP senators urging them to pass a more compassionate bill.

Here's one reason this should delight you and several that you should stay wary.

A number of "moderate" GOP reps voted for this bill even though they knew it was a political risk. Now their opponents, in addition to campaigning against them next year for voting for it, can cite the president calling their vote "mean" in their ads. It warms my heart to think of our local New Jersey Reps. MacArthur and Frelinghuysen feeling so betrayed this morning.

But be careful, Trump probably didn't mean this any more than he meant the words of praise for the bill he gave when he hosted the House GOP in the Rose Garden a few weeks ago. Politicians actually tell the truth far more often than they are given credit for. Trump almost never does. I feel like he doesn't even know what the truth is. He will praise whatever comes out of the Senate no matter how kind or mean it is and…

Any bill that comes out of the Senate will still be pretty damned mean. They aren't getting any Democratic votes for it so that means they have to keep Ted Cruz, Mike Lee, and Rand Paul happy (not to mention the many other very conservative senators). Don't let your guard down, defeating the Republican health-care bill is still going to be a huge fight.

But it's OK to enjoy their misery in the meantime.

JUNE 14, 2017: THOUGHTS ON SHOOTINGS AND POLITICAL RHETORIC

First off, let me make clear that I feel awful for the victims of today's shooting in Alexandria and deplore the actions of the shooter. Nothing justifies what he did.

As for the reaction to the shooting, well…

In 2011 Rep. Gabby Giffords was shot after appearing on a Sarah Palin advertisement with a target on her face.

In 2015, a man shot up a church in Charleston killing nine African Americans after a lifetime of hearing racist rhetoric.

In 1995 Timothy McVeigh blew up a government building in Oklahoma, killing more than one hundred. President Clinton correctly connected the bombing with the increasingly rancid antigovernment rhetoric coming from the right.

Is it possible that today's shooter decided to take action after hearing particularly hateful rhetoric about Trump and the Republicans? Yeah, it is. But the only people who have any standing to blame that rhetoric are those who also criticized Palin, racist politicians like David Duke, and the far right in the instances above. Otherwise, they should keep their traps shut. Because over the years, far right-wing rhetoric has led to far more of these incidents than far left-wing rhetoric.

As long as we have free speech and free guns in this country, terrorist attacks (can we please call this terrorism, it can be terrorism when a white guy does it) like what happened today is going to happen. And I'm not ready to give up free speech.

JUNE 16, 2017: WHERE IS THE REPUBLICAN BREAKING POINT?

When you come down to it, there is only one question that will determine the fate of the Trump presidency. At what point do the Republicans bail on Trump and start calling on him to resign? Here are the possibilities that I see.

a) After he fires Comey (OK scratch that one—clearly the wrong answer)
b) After he fires Mueller
c) After they fail to repeal Obamacare
d) After he tries to postpone the 2018 elections or declare martial law
e) Whenever his poll ratings fall below 30 percent
f) Never

What is your answer to this multiple-choice question?

JUNE 17, 2017: THE REPUBLICAN CALCULATION

This is a bit of a continuation of yesterday's post in response to some of the comments (here and on my personal page). Warning there is math (or at least lots of numbers).

There are roughly 240 Republican members of the House. The median district represented by a Republican voted roughly 60–40 for Trump (57–39 to be exact). Let's assume that district is 60 percent Republican.

Trump's current approval rating is between seventy-five and eighty among Republicans and around fifteen among Democrats. Making some assumptions about our median R District, Trump would win that district by about 54–46 today (down from 57–39). Our median Republican representative is better off sticking with Trump given his current approval ratings.

Now let's assume Trump's ratings go down to 30 percent overall, which probably corresponds to about 65–70 percent among Republicans and 5 percent among Democrats. Making the same assumptions as above Trump is losing that district by 56–44. Our median Republican representative should dump Trump, right?

Well not quite, because first he or she has to survive a primary, and 65–70 percent of Republicans are supporting Trump. So even at an approval rating of 30 percent, the risk to the Republican of losing their seat is greater in a primary (70–30) than in the general election (56–44).

A rough calculation says the break-even point (the point where the risk of losing in the general election because you support Trump is greater than losing in a primary because you dumped him) for the median Republican in the House is when Trump's approval ratings hit 25–26 percent. This means that when Trump falls to about this range, half of the Republicans in the House will be better off abandoning him then sticking with him.

Of course, you don't need half of the Republicans to abandon him because all of the Democrats will vote for impeachment. But you do need more Republicans than the number that would give impeachment a bare majority, because there is no way Paul Ryan would start impeachment hearings if only one-tenth of his caucus favored impeachment. You probably need somewhere between one-third and one-half of the Republican caucus to want to get rid of Trump to move forward. That means that the magic number for his poll ratings is higher than twenty-six but not by a lot. (As a reminder, Nixon was in the low twenties when he resigned.)

JUNE 19, 2017: WHERE DOES NOT NORMAL END UP?

I haven't done much NORMAL versus NOT NORMAL lately. Mostly that is because that very little in the headlines has been NORMAL (OK, maybe the plan to privatize air control or the announcement on apprenticeship programs). Instead, between the Russia investigation and the Senate attempt to repeal Obamacare in secret, all the big news has been NOT NORMAL.

Offline, a number of friends have told me that I'm too optimistic (there is no way he gets impeached) or too pessimistic (there is no way the worst-case scenarios can happen). In short, both of these viewpoints reflect the idea that the Trump administration will end NORMALly, he will lose reelection in 2020 (or not run), or he will win and we will have eight years of Trump followed by a NORMAL election in 2024.

It's a reasonable point of view and certainly one seemingly grounded in American experience up until this point. But consider this, of arguably the five worse presidencies ever (Buchanan, A. Johnson, Harding, Hoover, and Nixon), one ended in Civil War, one in the Great Depression, and two were plagued by impeachment. The most NORMAL conclusion was Harding who probably died of natural causes, but even there, there have always been rumors that his death was NOT NORMAL.

And Trump's presidency already promises to be less NORMAL than any of them (except maybe Nixon). And when you have a presidency where literally everything has been NOT NORMAL, my gut tells me that there is no way that its conclusion will be NORMAL. When Trump got elected, I told people his presidency would either end in authoritarianism or impeachment (or resignation). Everything that has happened since then has reinforced this view.

And everything we do (besides staving off disastrous policies like Obamacare repeal) should be focused on ensuring that the NOT NORMAL ending is impeachment or resignation in disgrace, because the alternative NOT NORMAL ending is awful.

JUNE 20, 2017: GEORGIA ON EVERYONE'S MIND

Here is your guide to interpreting the results of today's tossup special election in GA-6, which pits Republican Handel versus Democrat Ossoff for Tom Price's vacant seat.

Facts you need to know.

Price won this seat with 61, 66, and 65 percent in the last three elections.

Trump won this district by one point, but Romney and McCain won it by around twenty.

Ossoff will open a big early lead, perhaps by as much as fifteen points since early votes will favor him. Handel will spend the rest of the night closing the gap and possibly taking the lead.

The midterms are eighteen months away. There is very little predictive value in the outcome of this election for the midterms. The result tonight though may affect Republican behavior on health care and Trump. It may also inform the campaign next year and the types of candidates that the Democrats look for.

There are four possible outcomes as I see it, and here is how I will think about them.

Ossoff wins by more than five points: party time. The Democrats have won a major victory in a Republican district. Ossoff's strategy of running to the center has worked and may be a template for 2018. Republicans will panic.

Ossoff wins by one to five points: This is one of two likely outcomes. Democrats will rejoice over getting a win, and it will signify some movement toward them over the past six months. Ossoff's strategy is likely to be emulated.

Handel wins by one to five points: Sorry, this is also one of two likely outcomes. It is not out of line with polls, and it will still represent movement toward the Dems. But it will not be interpreted this way. There will be much hand wringing among Dems and rejoicing among Republicans despite the continued movement toward the Dems. There will be over-interpretations galore, as Berniecrats claim that centrists can't win and Republicans claim that we are still a center-right nation. All of these interpretations will be too broad to be supported by a single election result.

Handel wins by more than five points: Panic among Dems will be more justified. The movement toward the Dems that we saw in Montana and Kansas may have been temporary. The interpretations by the Berniecrats and the Republicans, although they are complete opposites and only one of them can be right, will deserve more attention.

This is the last election until November, which magnifies its importance. No one will have any other results to discuss until then, and it will affect the media narrative accordingly.

June 20, 2017: OK, that result sucked. But remember I said that it has virtually no predictive power for what will happen in 2018. So spend a day being depressed and then remember the words of the immortal Bluto[17] and get back out there and fight.

JUNE 22, 2017: FINAL THOUGHTS ON GEORGIA

I had hoped to be done with Georgia-06 by now, but the tendency on the left to self-flagellate is too great to ignore. I'll keep this brief. Keep the following things in mind when thinking about the election.

- In 2009, Democrats went five for five in special elections. They got obliterated in 2010.
- In 2012, Democrats held the presidency and the Senate. In 2008, Democrats held the House as well and had a filibuster proof majority in the Senate. The idea that Democrats can't win is ludicrous.
- There are seventy-one House districts represented by Republicans that are more favorable to Democrats than GA-06.
- As Dave Wasserman said, "Dems cleared 46% of 2-party vote in each of KS04, MTAL, GA06 & SC05. This indicates a *broad* House playing field, not a limited one."

While it is way too early to speculate about 2018, the path to victory is simple. Run candidates in every race. To the extent possible, make sure they look like their districts. No litmus tests except that they will fight Trump-Ryan-McConnell. And fight as if your country depended on it.

---

17 See https://www.youtube.com/watch?v=V8lT1o0sDwI.

JUNE 24, 2017: MCCONNELL'S STRATEGY

On Thursday Mitch McConnell released the text of the reprehensible Republican health-care bill. Now the speculation turns to whether it will pass in a vote next week. If it does, the repeal of Obamacare, and frankly more importantly the gutting of Medicaid, becomes likely (it would then go back to the House for a vote).

McConnell needs fifty votes. There are forty-eight Democrats, none of whom will vote for the bill. That means McConnell can spare no more than two Republican votes. Earlier this week, four very conservative Republican Senators (Paul, Cruz, Lee, and Johnson) said the bill wasn't awful enough for them. Dean Heller (R-NV) the most vulnerable Republican in 2018 also announced his opposition.

Here is how I think this goes:

1. The bill gets amended on the floor to ensure that other "moderate" Republicans are OK with it. My guess is that the Planned Parenthood and abortion provisions get taken out (the abortion one may get ruled out of bounds by the Senate parliamentarian saving the Republicans the political cost of getting rid of it) to win over Murkowski and Collins. More opioid money will be added to woo Portman and Capito.
2. McConnell is OK with Heller and one other Republican defecting (Flake, Cassidy, or one of the ones mentioned above).
3. McConnell then dares the conservatives to vote against it and torpedo Obamacare repeal.
4. McConnell is actually probably fine if the bill passes (he gets to claim credit) or fails (he can blame the senators he hates the most and not have to worry about electoral backlash). Then he gets to move on to tax cuts, which is his top priority.

Two takeaways:

Don't play poker with Mitch McConnell.

Call your senators. Especially Murkowski, Collins, Heller, Flake, Portman, and Capito.

June 26, 2017: Great article on Nixon-Watergate versus Trump-Russia.[18] Money quote:

What's more likely is that the Trump administration will continue to mirror Garry Wills's description of Nixon's: "a world of little men using large powers incompetently from a combination of suspicion and panic." The little men will continue to drive the country into a ditch. And GOP leaders will look the other way right up to that moment when Republicans in the 60 to 80 districts (according to FiveThirtyEight) more competitive than those in last week's special elections figure out that they may have to choose between the minority of voters who are Trump's irreducible base and a larger group, including Independents, who will determine whether they keep their jobs.

JUNE 27, 2017: HEALTH CARE IS COMPLICATED; THIS BILL IS SIMPLE

The CBO score of the Senate health-care bill came out last night and lo and behold CBO projects that twenty-two million people will lose their health insurance over the next ten years. Numbers have power, so it is great to have the twenty-two million to toss around, but the intent of this bill was clear long before CBO got their hands on it.

It is a redistribution of health, wealth, and welfare from the least fortunate to the most fortunate. Nothing more, nothing less.

Politics (particularly on domestic issues) is, more than anything else, about how we decide to distribute well-being in society. Over the course of American history, there have been redistributions up the income scale before (the W. Bush and Reagan tax cuts come to mind). But nothing comes close to this one in magnitude. Overtime we have expanded the American Dream to more and more people. Obamacare was one step in that process. Repealing it (and gutting Medicaid) would be a bigger step backward from this dream, than I think we have ever taken.

This shouldn't be a close call. But it is. Keep calling.

---

18 Frank Rich, "Just Wait: Watergate Didn't Become Watergate Overnight Either," *New York*, June 25, 2017, http://nymag.com/daily/intelligencer/2017/06/frank-rich-nixon-trump-and-how-a-presidency-ends.html.

JUNE 28, 2017: VICTORY (OR DEFEAT DEFERRED)?

Back when I worked at OMB, one of my colleagues would cynically comment that a defeat deferred counted as a victory (we lost a lot of internal bureaucratic battles).

Unfortunately, with the Senate health-care vote, we don't have that luxury. Yesterday's news that the Senate will not vote on its Obamacare repeal before the July 4 recess was good news. But the fight is not over. Those of you in Ohio, West Virginia, Maine, Alaska, Louisiana, Nevada, and Colorado need to continue reaching out to your Senators over the recess. Because the bill may come back.

Indeed, everyone hopefully remembers the thrill of Paul Ryan pulling the House health-care bill in March only to see it passed six weeks later. McConnell likely hopes for the same outcome. Two things will make his job harder than Ryan's:

1. He has fewer votes to spare.
2. With a vote on the debt ceiling coming up and budget season nearly upon us, he has less time than Ryan had. There are thirty-two Senate session days left before he can no longer use reconciliation.

Still, remain vigilant. Enjoy yesterday's victory, and make sure it is not a defeat deferred.

JUNE 30, 2017: THIS IS WHO HE IS

There was a lot of attention yesterday paid to Trump's tweets about Mika Brzezinski. I did not pay a lot of attention to it. This isn't to say that everything that people said—"It was appalling," "It was sexist," "It was beneath the dignity of the office"—wasn't true. It was. What it wasn't, was news.

Before he was a candidate, he was a racist, sexist, self-aggrandizing monomaniac. During the campaign he insulted the disabled, a Mexican judge, Muslims, African Americans, and most frequently, women. I mean, we had a tape saying he'd grab women by the xxxxx. We should be surprised by his tweets? As president (as one person on Twitter put it), he has shown that there is no floor to the dignity of the office.

Frankly, for those who are still with him, you have effectively endorsed all of these behaviors. And for those politicians that continue to carry his water (while doing no more than expressing concern), this goes triple for you. And boy, do I hope I live to see his enablers pay the political consequences for the damnation they have visited upon the body politic.

JULY 3, 2017: WHILE HE WAS TWEETING

The biggest news on Friday barely got reported. Mitch McConnell, not giving up on repealing Obamacare, sent two bills to CBO for scores. His hope is to get the scores from CBO before the Senate returns from its July 4 recess a week from today and then take one more run at passing a bill.

No one knows what is in the bills (one reportedly includes the "Cruz option" which would allow insurers to offer plans that don't meet Obamacare standards as long as they offer one plan that does). My guess is that the bills are both awful.

Trump's tweets dominated the airwaves. I don't think Trump is doing it on purpose to distract people, I think he is doing whatever he feels like at a given moment. But McConnell is very happy to have the attention elsewhere. The reception that Senators Portman, Capito, Collins, Heller, Cassidy, and Flake get at home this week will be very important.

JULY 5, 2017: TRUMP ELECTION COMMISSION REQUEST ILLEGAL (APPEARED IN THE *REGULATORY REVIEW*)[19]

Recently, the newly created Presidential Advisory Commission on Election Integrity sent a letter to all fifty states asking them to submit extensive information about registered voters. The letter has created an uproar among state officials, and many have announced their intention to refuse the request. President Donald Trump has tweeted his disapproval of these state refusals.

---

19 Stuart Shapiro, "Voter Data Request is Illegal, Not Just Controversial," *The Regulatory Review*, July 5, 2017, https://www.theregreview.org/2017/07/05/shapiro-voter-request-illegal-controversial/.

Overlooked in the controversy has been the rather obvious conclusion that, because the Commission on Election Integrity appears to have ignored the requirements of the Paperwork Reduction Act (PRA), its request is simply illegal.

The PRA was passed in 1980 with bipartisan support and signed by President Jimmy Carter. A central purpose of the law was to ensure that, before collecting information from the American public, federal agencies solicited public comment and received approval from the Office of Information and Regulatory Affairs (OIRA). In the thirty-seven years since the passage of the PRA, tens of thousands of government information collections have gone through this process.

Yet the commission's request letter did not include any indication that it had been submitted for review through the PRA process. The PRA requires not only that OIRA review requests for information but also that agencies include on any such request an approval number and an estimate of the time it will take for a respondent to provide the information requested.

The PRA and its implementing regulations do include exceptions to its public comment and OIRA approval requirements, but the request for voter data does not seem to meet any of those exceptions. To wit, the commission is a federal agency under the definition in the PRA's implementing regulations. It has clearly requested information, specifically:

the full first and last names of all registrants, middle names or initials if available, addresses, dates of birth, political party (if recorded in your state), last four digits of social security number if available, voter history (elections voted in) from 2006 onward, active or inactive status, canceled status, information regarding any felony convictions, information regarding voter registration in another state, information regarding military status, and overseas citizen information.

And the same information was presumably requested of ten or more entities—fifty in this case.

Under the PRA, the commission must calculate the burden on state officials of complying with the information request. The commission must also explain how it will protect and eventually dispose of the information.

Perhaps most importantly, given the uproar the letter has generated, the commission must also explain why the government needs the information and how it will be used.

Agencies across the government have regularly bemoaned the PRA, and how it makes their jobs harder. Indeed, there are cases where agencies must wait months to collect information that everyone agrees is useful and on which no member of the public will ever submit comments. But in cases where the government is imposing a significant burden on the public or collecting sensitive data, the PRA is an important safeguard against government overreach.

The commission's letter calls for exactly the type of information collection with which the PRA was enacted to deal. In such a sensitive policy area involving the sanctity of voting privacy and the legitimacy of elections, public comment is particularly important. Further, OIRA review focuses specifically on how the government will use the information and whether that use justifies the burden on the American public. These questions go to the heart of the issues surrounding the commission's request.

For these reasons, the commission should immediately withdraw its request for voter data. If it decides it still wants to proceed to ask states for these data, it should start over and follow the requirements of the PRA. Only then will a transparent and thoughtful review of this highly controversial collection of information take place, as contemplated under federal law.

JULY 6, 2017: UPDATE ON ELECTION COMMISSION

Yesterday I blogged about how the request from the Presidential Advisory Commission on Election Integrity for voter data violated the Paperwork Reduction Act. The blog post (originally on the *Regulatory Review*) got quite a bit of attention.

- With some help from my friends, it got picked up by the *Hill* and was their lead story.
- It then got picked up by other media sources across the country.

- The press secretary for VP Pence denied that the request was illegal because the commission was not an "agency." According to almost everyone I've spoken with, he is wrong.
- Meanwhile there is another collection from the Department of Justice that went out the same day as the voter data, one that may also violate the PRA.[20]

JULY 7, 2017: STAYING OR GOING

Yesterday the head of the Office of Government Ethics, Walter Shaub, resigned. He decided he could do more outside the government than he was accomplishing inside it (obviously this administration has not cared about ethics). He may be right.

But Shaub has the luxury of resigning. He'll get a good job and lots of speaking opportunities. The tens of thousands who work within the executive branch (including some friends of mine) don't have it so easy. They have job security and families to support, and some are close to earning generous pensions for years of service to their country. They are confronted with an occupying army above them that in many cases despises them and everything they stand for.

Marissa Golden, a political scientist, who wrote about federal employees during the Reagan administration, characterizes civil servants who object to the views of their political superiors as having four choices: exit, which means doing what Shaub did yesterday; voice, argue with your superiors, at the risk of being cut out of decisions; neglect, do the minimum necessary to keep your job; and loyalty, do what your superiors ask (within constraints of course). All of these have their costs, some professional, some ethical, some both.

So keep these people in mind in the months ahead. Here are some of their stories.[21]

---

20 See https://www.documentcloud.org/documents/3881855-Correspondence-DOJ-Letter-06282017.html

21 Marin Cogan and Nick Tabor, "Should they Stay or Should they Go? Federal Employees Talk About the Ethics of Sticking it Out with the Trump Administration," *New York Magazine*, July 5, 2017, http://nymag.com/daily/intelligencer/2017/07/6-federal-employees-on-sticking-it-out-in-the-trump-era.html.

JULY 8, 2017: MORE RUSSIA

Since Trump had his annual performance review with Putin yesterday, it is a good time to remind everyone why we have to keep screaming Russia at every opportunity (while screaming health care, climate, and so on—we have to do a lot of screaming).

1. Below[22], a reminder that Trump has already done enough to make us believe he encouraged and possibly assisted Russian hacking in 2018. Key quote, "But whatever happened out of public view, the existing record is already conclusively shameful. Trump and his crew were active enablers of Putin's operation to subvert an American election. That is fire, not smoke. That is scandal enough."

Then, a reminder that Trump has already done enough to be accused of obstruction of justice.[23] Key quote, "Under such a plain legal analysis, of the sort my students and I conduct in the law school classroom, it is highly likely that special counsel Robert Mueller will find that there is a provable case that the president committed a federal felony offense."

And finally,[24] a reminder that Trump wants to see Russian interference in the 2018 elections. Key quote, "It is far more parsimonious to assume that the man who asked Russia to intervene against his opponent at a press conference a year ago is, in a subtler but more insidious way, inviting a repeat performance next year and in 2020."

JULY 9, 2017: SO MUCH WINNING

As one sees our standing (and the standing of democracy and freedom) in the world plummet and immigrants in our communities deported, it is not

---

22 David Corn, "We Already Know Trump Betrayed America," *Mother Jones*, July 8, 2017., http://www.motherjones.com/politics/2017/05/trump-putin-russia-scandal-guilty/.

23 David Buell, "Open and Shut," *Slate*, July 2017, http://www.slate.com/articles/news_and_politics/jurisprudence/2017/07/the_obstruction_of_justice_case_against_trump_is_already_a_slam_dunk.html.

24 Brian Beutler, "Trump Wants Russia to Interfere for Him Again," *The New Republic*, July 7, 2017, https://newrepublic.com/article/143753/trump-wants-russia-interfere.

unreasonable to bemoan where we are as a country and to wonder if it will ever get better. In times like this, it is important to remember the victories of the past six months.

- Despite having control of the presidency and both houses of Congress, Republicans have not passed one major bill.
- This includes a failure to date to deliver on their promise to repeal Obamacare.
- The Trump administration has lost repeatedly in court. From the original travel ban being thrown out to the decision this week, disallowing an attempt to repeal regulations on methane emissions, it has been one loss after another.
- Trump's approval rating has been below 40 percent for months.
- And most importantly, six months into his presidency, Trump is under investigation for allegations that amount to treason.

Why has all this happened? Because of good people in the media, in Congress, and in the judiciary. But also because of marches, calls to offices, and donations to groups that sue the administration and organize the resistance. Because of you.

I don't mean to minimize the damage Trump has done. I still fear the outcome of this presidency and think that even if he left tomorrow, it will take years to undo the damage he's done. But it could be much worse. And it isn't—because what's best about America has stood up to what's worst about America.

JULY 10, 2017: IT COULDN'T HAPPEN TO A NICER HEIR

There were so many things I was going to write about today. Then the *NY Times* forced me to scrap those with their revelation that Donald Trump Jr. (an aside: other than Dad, is there a member of the family whose downfall you'd rather see than Junior?) organized a meeting with a Russian lawyer with deep ties to the Russian government with the purpose of getting information on Hillary Clinton. Junior basically confirmed this.

There are many interpretations of this going around the Interwebs (Junior is an idiot, Junior is taking the fall for Manafort and Kushner who were also at the meeting, Junior is still lying—note these are not mutually exclusive). But no matter how you slice it, Junior is in deep, deep trouble. And two days after Trump talked about moving forward on the Russia scandal, he's got to be pretty worried himself.

As Dan Rather (a fantastic follow on both Facebook and Twitter by the way) said, just as we wondered forty-five years ago, so we should be asking now, "What did the president know, and when did he know it?"

And we should also be asking, "What did the vice president know, and when did he know it?"

JULY 12, 2017: ETHICS, POLITICS, LAW, AND DONALD TRUMP JR.

As you all know, yesterday we received concrete evidence that Donald Trump Jr. met with a Russian agent after hearing that she might have information on Hillary Clinton. This isn't a rumor and cannot be dismissed as fake news since Junior himself turned over the e-mails. So what does it mean?

Let's start with the easiest question. By agreeing to meet with the Russians and expressing enthusiasm about securing their help, Junior did something unambiguously wrong. If you can't recognize that agreeing to meet with a foreign power that has interests around the globe that run contrary not only to ours but to those of freedom, tolerance, and democracy and hoping they will help you is wrong, then I have no use for your opinions on anything further on this matter. Regardless of the law, Junior betrayed this country.

Now it gets harder. The legal definition of treason is, "Whoever, owing allegiance to the United States, levies war against them or adheres to their enemies, giving them aid and comfort within the United States or elsewhere, is guilty of treason and shall suffer death, or shall be imprisoned not less than five years and fined under this title but not less than $10,000; and shall be incapable of holding any office under the United States." It's not clear that Junior committed treason in a legal sense.

As for campaign-finance laws, the relevant law prohibits "receiving" a "contribution or donation" of "money or other thing of value" in connection with an election. So the legality hangs here on whether information is some "thing of value." I don't know of any litigation history on this.

So it is not yet clear that Trump Jr. is in legal trouble (he may be...I'm not a lawyer). But the key word is "yet." First of all there are probably more revelations coming. If anyone has a tape of the conversation between Junior and the Russian and it is clear that the information was offered in exchange for relieving sanctions, that would be illegal. If there are more e-mails indicating a quid pro quo, that would be illegal. If he is put under oath (a virtual certainty) and lies about his actions, he is in legal trouble for perjury. So, while it is not yet clear he is in trouble, it is very clear he will be soon.

That brings us to politics. In the end, this crisis has to be resolved politically. Republicans want you to focus on the legal implications of Junior's actions, not the ethical ones. Don't. But hopefully soon it won't matter. As with every other development in this crisis, the revelations of the past few days tighten the noose further on Trump Sr. The clear wrongdoing here will erode his support a bit further, and the likely legal problems soon to come for his son will weaken it even more. Then the end comes closer.

JULY 14, 2017: BACK TO HEALTH CARE

In the ping pong of stories of critical importance, it is time to go back to health care from Russia. McConnell released his revised bill yesterday. A CBO score will come early next week. And then a vote on the motion to proceed. This vote is the best chance to stop the bill; once they start debating it, its chances of passing go up.

The new bill is not much better than the previous versions. There (as predicted) is some opioid money and a carve-out for Alaska. Some of the tax cuts for the wealthy are gone (the biggest improvement in my view). But the core of the bill is still the gutting of Medicaid. No one should pretend it is about anything else.

Susan Collins and Rand Paul immediately came out against it. This means that one more vote is enough to defeat the motion. But here's the thing. You won't get just one more vote. You'll get either four or five votes, which will lead to McConnell pulling the bill again before a vote. Or you won't get any, and it will pass 51–50.

Heller (NV) and Flake (AZ) are the most vulnerable incumbents up for election next year. Call and tell them (if you can) that you will donate to their opponents if they vote for the motion. Portman (OH), Capito (WV), Murkowski (AK), Gardner (CO), and Cassidy (LA) are also on the fence. If you live in their states, call.

JULY 16, 2017: THE PROBLEM WITH AMATEURS

An underestimated problem (yes, not the biggest problem) with Trump's election is that it represents the culmination of years of fetishizing outsiders in politics. Politics and governance are skills. Trump doesn't know the first thing about either (although he learned some things about politics during the campaign, he still knows nothing about governing).

On the one hand that is helping us in his inability to help Congress pass its Obamacare repeal and his repeated failures in the courts. On the other hand, it is damaging faith in government and destroying our reputation abroad. Here is a great article[25] that explains why "outsiders" don't belong in top political positions (and I don't know why Howard Dean is pictured).

JULY 17, 2017: WHAT KEEPS ME UP AT NIGHT

It's not Russia or health care or climate change (although God knows all of those are scary). It's the one thing that could make changes in all of them permanent. Voter suppression has a dark history in this country, and some are trying to learn from history and repeat it.

This is a battle that will be fought in states and localities far away from where many of us global elites live. The story below[26] talks about Mississippi in particular and the south in general. Read it when you have time.

---

25 Julia Azari, "Political Amateurs are a Threat to Democracy," *Vox.com*, July 12, 2017, https://www.vox.com/mischiefs-of-faction/2017/7/12/15959032/political-amateurs-threat-to-democracy.

26 Pema Levy, "These Three Lawyers are Quietly Purging Voter Rolls Across the Country," *Mother Jones*, July 7, 2017, http://www.motherjones.com/politics/2017/07/these-three-lawyers-are-quietly-purging-voter-rolls-across-the-country/.

JULY 18, 2017: SCENARIO UPDATE

Early in the Trump presidency, I outlined four ways it would progress and end (and then later added a fifth). Here is an update on how the likelihood of each outcome has moved.

1) A gradual march toward Trump's ouster (impeachment or resignation). I initially listed this as the most likely outcome. Since then he has fired the FBI director investigating his campaign, and revelations have come out that his son met with Russians saying they had information on his opponent. So, yeah, I'd say the likelihood of this one has gone up (since I had it high to begin with, it may not have climbed much, but it has climbed).

2) A sudden Trump departure. This is based on his unpredictability. He is just as unpredictable as he was on day one. This one has held steady (but far behind #1).

3) Authoritarianism. I still believe this is Trump-Bannon's desired outcome. What I failed to appreciate is that while Trump is intellectually and temperamentally inclined to be a dictator, he is not intellectually or temperamentally inclined to gradually attack institutions and accumulate power. In other words he is more Kim Jong Un (without being born to power) than Erdogan or Chavez. Still a major terrorist attack keeps this possibility live though lower than in November.

4) A typical Republican presidency. Suffice to say this one has fallen off the charts. I still think Congress will pass a tax cut for the wealthy and a budget that hurts the poor (but not nearly as much as Trump's proposal). Still in most other areas, this presidency has been NOT NORMAL, and I don't think its progression or conclusion will be NORMAL either.

5) Four years of chaos. This was the extra scenario I introduced after January. This is the other big mover upward (besides #1). This presidency has progressed from one NOT NORMAL event to another. And at this point, it is fair to say it will continue as long as he is president.

I think we have moved to a world where #1 and #5 have opened up big leads on the other three scenarios.

JULY 19, 2017: POLITICS MATTERS…BARELY

Yesterday a bill that would have deprived tens of millions of people of tangible benefits while helping a much smaller group of people died in the Senate…and it was front page news. Anyone who has ever studied politics could tell you the Obamacare repeal was a political loser. The question is why did it get so close to passing?

The gut reaction on much of the left is that it must be because of powerful moneyed interests. But that doesn't work here. There were plenty of powerful moneyed interests in favor of Obamacare including the insurance companies who got tons of customers from it. Sure, the Koch brothers didn't like it, but why could they almost overpower not only the masses but the special interests?

Basically I think the only explanation that holds water is the power of Obama hatred. This was his signature program. For seven years, Republican candidates selfishly and deceitfully convinced their voters that they didn't benefit from Obamacare but that undeserving people (read: minorities) did. Obamacare regularly polled as less popular than the Affordable Care Act or than the individual components of the law.

They managed to create an image of Obamacare that mirrored Reagan's use of welfare queens in the 1970s and 1980s. But at the end of the day, the fact that enough of their constituents realized that they would lose health insurance if the Republicans got their way saved Obamacare. It was much closer than it should have been though.

JULY 20, 2017: WHERE TRUMP CAN DO DAMAGE DOMESTICALLY

With the failure of the Obamacare repeal in Congress (or near-failure since they are trying to resurrect it yet again) and court setbacks galore, it is tempting to gloat at the incompetence of the Trump administration. But besides the damage they can do in foreign policy where the president has huge power, there are areas of domestic policy where very bad things are happening.

The article below[27] describes one of them. It talks about how immigration policy is being used to discriminate against Muslims even in the absence of the travel ban. Another example is in the first comment, which describes how AG Sessions has implemented draconian procedures on asset forfeiture of individuals *suspected* of a crime. Finally if the Obamacare repeal fails, Trump has threatened to undermine it administratively (well, he used shorter words) by actions at HHS and IRS.

All of these are within his power. Over the past several decades, presidential power has grown due to actions by presidents of both parties and negligence by Congresses controlled by both parties. The result is an executive who can do a great deal of damage (or good but that's not relevant here) and do so in ways that will attract little attention and leave little recourse.

JULY 22, 2017: THE QUICKENING

The news this year has come faster and more furiously than ever before (even faster than during the 2016 campaign). But some weeks are particularly crazy. The week that Comey was fired and Mueller was appointed held the record for most insane (as measured by the number of times I check my Twitter feed). Last week when Junior's meetings with half of Russia were revealed was pretty big too.

But this week can stand with any of them. Trumps interview, more revelations about the meeting with Junior, revelations about Trump's second meeting with Putin, Spicer's resignation, Kasowitz's resignation, Trump's asking about whether he can pardon himself and his family, and yesterday the revelation that Sessions met with Kislyak during the campaign.

---

27 Farhana Kehra and Jonathan J. Smith, "How Trump is Stealthily Carrying Out his Muslim Ban," *New York Times*, July 18, 2017, https://www.nytimes.com/2017/07/18/opinion/trump-muslim-ban-supreme-court.html?_r=0.

Sometimes things calm down again. But this feels different. The Republicans in Congress most likely now realize that Obamacare repeal is not happening, so Trump's usefulness to them has decreased. Trump's ratings are trickling down. Putin must realize he's not getting his sanctions relief. Trump realizes all of this too (I don't give him credit for much, but he must know that the noose is tightening).

It feels like a crisis is coming (I mean a really big one). Trump fires Mueller, or Trump pardons a family member. And then the hellmouth opens (*Buffy the Vampire Slayer* reference).

JULY 23, 2017: OBAMACARE UPDATE

Yesterday I characterized Obamacare repeal by saying it was "most likely… not happening." I stand by the characterization but remind everyone that this bill is like the *Terminator* (in more senses than one). It won't die. Remember that "mostly dead" means "slightly alive." Mitch McConnell intends to force a vote on a "motion to proceed" this week. He expects it to fail and then for conservative backlash to frighten moderate Republican senators into later changing their votes.

It is a strategy that reflects desperation. But that doesn't mean there is no chance it will work. That means more phone calls. Call your senators (especially if they are Heller, Murkowski, Capito, Cassidy, Portman, and Gardner) and tell them to vote against the motion to proceed. Then keep them on your speed dial as they start to feel pressure from the Tea Party.

JULY 24, 2017: OBAMACARE UPDATE (AGAIN)

Chances of this passing are slowly going up. Rumors are that Senator McCain will be flown in for the vote, which they wouldn't be doing if it wasn't going to be close. I could go on and on about the vileness of passing this bill without committee hearings or even revealing publicly what is in the bill. I could go on and on about the hypocrisy of any Republican who spoke out about against this bill and the process by which it was developed and now might vote for it.

Instead I just called Senators Heller and Flake and told them I'll be donating to their opponents next year if they vote yes on the motion to proceed tomorrow (Tuesday). Call them, and do the same if you can afford to donate. Call your senators if they are on the fence or haven't yet stated a position (again the list is Capito (WV), Portman (OH), Murkowski (AK), Gardner (CO), and Cassidy (LA)).

JULY 25, 2017: SICKENING HEALTH-CARE VOTE BUT NO TIME TO GET SICK

Just watched the Senate vote on the motion to proceed on the debate over Obamacare. It passed 51–50 with Collins and Murkowski voting no, and VP Pence needed to break the tie.

That fifty senators would vote to proceed on a bill that does not yet exist and would likely hurt many of their constituents violates everything the Senate and arguably representative democracy stands for. Capito (WV) said she wouldn't vote to proceed on repeal unless she was confident that a replacement would pass. She voted to proceed without a replacement defined. The examples of hypocrisy like this (including I hate to say it, McCain's farewell speech) abounded today.

However, there will be plenty of time to hammer the Republicans if the eventual bill passes. Now it is time to fight. This isn't over yet. The chances of Obamacare repeal passing have gone up a good deal, but they are nowhere near 100 percent. A series of tweets from Chris Hayes[28] points out that outright repeal and the original replacement are likely doomed, but "skinny repeal" might pass. What is skinny repeal? No one knows yet.

JULY 27, 2017: ON DISTRACTION AND OUTRAGE

There is a nice column in the *New York Times* today[29] about how Trump is exhausting our capacity for outrage by doing and saying so many awful things. Just this week he has

---

28 See tweets at: https://twitter.com/chrislhayes/status/889926438366978048

29 Peter Baker, "Trump White House Tests a Nation's Capacity for Outrage," *New York Times*, July 24, 2017, https://www.nytimes.com/2017/07/24/us/politics/attorney-general-bush-trump.html.

- tweeted that he is banning transgender individuals from the military,
- called for his opponent in the last election to be investigated,
- publicly humiliated his attorney general (I'm all for humiliating Jeff Sessions—but I didn't pick him to be AG), and
- made a speech in front of the Boy Scouts that set new lows for inappropriateness.

And it is still early Thursday morning.

You know what, they are all **NOT NORMAL** and outrageous. They are all worth your anger. They all hurt this country by lowering the expected behavior of government officials in general and the president in particular. Respect for the office will take a generation to recover if it ever does. And that respect was one of our greatest assets.

But at the same time, there are even bigger things to be outraged about. I have chosen to focus most of my attention on the Russia scandal and health care because I believe the first may be an existential threat to democracy in this country (and the best hope of removing Trump who is himself such a threat) and the latter because of the sheer magnitude of the number of people who would be hurt by it. But it is hard to stay focused when the president behaves like your crazy uncle and his administration hurts people in other ways.

Then I remember that previous generations came across oceans to make a new life here, fought the Nazis, fought against slavery and for civil rights, and protested the Vietnam War. And paying attention to everything, calling my senators regularly, and writing as much as possible about what I see, doesn't seem like much of a big deal. So give it your best shot, Trump; we're here to fight your outrages and your distractions on every front.

JULY 28, 2017: HEROES AND OTHER COMPLICATED FIGURES

John McCain provided the decisive vote last night killing the Obamacare repeal effort (for now). John McCain gave us Sarah Palin. He fought tirelessly for campaign-finance reform. He has cast dozens of votes I think were awful. Most American political figures who survive for a long time have complicated legacies. John McCain is certainly one of them.

Lisa Murkowski and Susan Collins deserve at least as much praise as McCain. They stayed firm against repeal despite being insulted and threatened by members of their own party. They too have done things I strongly disagree with, but they were heroes in this battle.

The Democrats stayed unified throughout the fight. From Bernie Sanders to Joe Manchin, the unwieldy Democratic caucus spoke as one. Huge praise to Charles Schumer who was the key figure in making that happen.

The Trump administration will now continue to try and weaken Obamacare from within. The danger here is real but that shouldn't blind us to the much greater danger that has just passed.

Now let's get this bastard out of the presidency.

JULY 31, 2017: TRUMP AND THE GOP

In the past week, Trump

- fired Reince Priebus and Sean Spicer, both long-time Republican party hacks;
- threatened Lisa Murkowski using his Secretary of the Interior Ryan Zinke; and
- continually harangued Republicans in the Senate "ordering" them to do away with the filibuster and resume work on the Obamacare repeal.

There has been speculation (including in the articles below) that Trump is casting himself away from the Republican Party. Bannon's ideology of populist authoritarianism never lined up well with the more corporatist libertarian ethos of Republican leaders so this would make some sense, except...

The Republican Party is all that is protecting Trump from possible impeachment right now. If he turns on them, he gives them one less reason to stick up for him in Congress. Those who have doubted my argument that impeachment is an eventual possibility continually cite the Republicans in Congress. What if Trump turns on them, starts going after them more in the press, recruits people to run against them in 2018 primaries? He couldn't be that stupid…could he?

AUGUST 1, 2017: TRUMP'S WAR ON ANALYSIS (ORIGINALLY APPEARED IN THE HILL)[30]

President Donald Trump has brought many crusades to Washington.

One that has received less attention than his pledges to "drain the swamp" and his jeremiads against illegal immigration is his administration's systematic attempts to discredit objective analysis of policy problems.

This "war on analysis" has also spread to portions of the Republican establishment that have historically been among the advocates for an analytical approach to policy.

Support for policy analysis in general, and cost-benefit analysis in particular, has always been somewhat bipartisan, but many of its strongest advocates have been Republican.

The idea that we should analyze the potential impacts of a policy and evaluate them after they have been in place has been seen as a way to ensure that when the government intervenes in the market, it does so carefully and it pulls back when errors are made.

But in a number of instances, the Trump administration has abandoned these principles. Most prominently have been the battles over the Congressional Budget Office scores of the various Obamacare replacements considered by Congress.

---

30 Stuart Shapiro, "Trump Still Ignoring Facts but Numbers Don't Lie," *The Hill*, August 1, 2017, http://thehill.com/blogs/pundits-blog/the-administration/344798-tell-trump-numbers-dont-lie-how-the-president-ignores#bottom-story-socials.

The Trump White House has called these analyses "fake news." This has led to legislation in the House, which would fundamentally alter CBO's mission and move it away from analysis. All of this because Trump and fellow Republicans didn't like the results of CBO's analysis.

Another example is the Trump administration attempt to repeal the Environmental Protection Agency "Waters of the United States" regulation. In its economic analysis, EPA simply ignored numerous categories of benefits that the original regulation would have created.

One economist who has worked for industry to repeal or modify the regulation called the analysis "the worst regulatory analysis I have ever seen."

Finally the administration's entire approach to regulation shows a disdain for analysis. The centerpiece of this approach was the president's "two for one" executive order, requiring agencies to eliminate two regulations before promulgating a new one.

The order ignores the longstanding bipartisan commitment to cost-benefit analysis of significant regulations. Trump's approach has largely been applauded and its anti-analytical approach ignored by Republicans.

The war on analysis is part of a broader war on expertise of all kinds. From ignoring scientists to deriding government produced statistics, the Trump administration has tried to sow doubts of any numbers that raise questions about their policies.

Honest policy analysis makes no pretension to giving us the "right" answer to a public-policy problem. The same is true of economics more broadly. Nor does honest analysis prescribe a particular solution to a policy question.

But good analysis is part of a commitment to give better answers to these challenging issues. It is a way of ensuring that political leaders make decisions only after seeing the best information possible. And ignoring or devaluing this analysis is a sign that "better" answers are not of interest to political decision-makers.

In the absence of analysis, we are left with the gut feelings of political decision-makers or their appointees. And while there is some chance that those gut feelings are informed by noble intentions, they may also be informed by conscious or unconscious biases or the information that these decision-makers have been given by lobbyists.

Elevating good analysis is a way of draining the swamp. Ignoring good analysis is a way of propagating its stench.

AUGUST 2, 2017: A NOT NORMAL FORTY-EIGHT HOURS

In the past two days:

- It was revealed that Trump's "beleaguered" AG Sessions may be beginning an investigation into discrimination against white people in college admissions (seriously, WTF!).
- Nominal Secretary of State Tillerson spurned $80 million earmarked to counter ISIS and Russian propaganda.
- Politico released a transcript of a *Wall Street Journal* interview with Trump that the journal suppressed (presumably because Trump sounds like a fool).
- A lawsuit revealed accusations that *Fox News* concocted the Seth Rich story, possibly with help directly from the White House.
- Trump has worked with conservative senators to draft legislation that would limit legal immigration. Meanwhile Stephen Miller has been spouting anti-immigrant canards on the air.
- A Flynn appointee was knocked off the National Security Council. This is the third Flynn-Bannon ally in a month that McMaster has purged.

The only NORMAL thing that happened was that Trump signed the Russia sanctions bill and issued a signing statement arguing that parts of the bill were unconstitutional (any president would have done the same). The petulant press release that accompanied the signing statement though was NOT NORMAL.

We continue to be governed by someone with the emotional maturity of a child with no understanding of his job. Like a child he wants absolute control. Meanwhile beneath him, there is clearly a battle going on between the white supremacist Bannon wing and the generals (McMaster and Kelly).

But Trump's approval ratings are dropping. That's the key to everything. Just keep pushing. Hopefully all of this NOT NORMAL stuff will keep pushing it down.

AUGUST 4, 2017: A GRAND (JURY) DAY

Since lawyers can explain the legal implications of the news that Mueller has convened a grand jury better than I can, I leave it to Seth Abrahamson in his tweetstorm.[31] I'll focus on the political implications here.

- If Trump fires Mueller now, he basically is inviting Obstruction of Justice charges. His allies in Congress (they are fewer and fewer each day, and firing Mueller will erode the number further) can forestall the reinstatement of Mueller for a while, but the clock will be ticking on impeachment.
- Of course, if Trump is guilty of collusion or if he knows Mueller is close to something else, he still may be better off firing Mueller and taking his chances. Note that Hannity has called for Mueller to be replaced.
- The dog whistles to the alt-right this week (Miller's interview and Trump's plan to curb legal immigration) were now in retrospect attempts to shore up his base in preparation for the bad news he knew was coming.
- Grand juries take time, often a year or more, so on the one hand there may be a lot of time for this to play out. But other sources have said subpoenas have already been issued. So Mueller (conscious of the precarious position he is in) may be moving faster than usual.
- Graham's bill to protect Mueller is another sign that Trump is bleeding Republicans. I can't emphasize enough how NOT NORMAL it is for the president's party to be abandoning him this early in his

---

31 See tweetstorm at https://twitter.com/SethAbramson/status/893206561316909056.

administration. They will come back if he can improve his approval ratings, but he clearly has not figured out how to do this.

The noose got one notch tighter yesterday. Happy vacation, Mr. President.

AUGUST 5, 2017: WHERE I GET MY NEWS

For those of us obsessed with politics, we are now inundated with news sources. The Internet has democratized the provision of information, but most new sources of info provide no quality control. For that reason, when it comes to trusting information, I tend to rely on what is often describe derogatorily as the "mainstream media" (although in reaction to Trump, more people are thankfully calling it the free press).

The free press has some major advantages over your typical blogger or "citizen journalist" in providing facts. They don't publish something until they have tried to verify it. Their reporters are trained in journalism, which is a discipline that still has a set of norms (admittedly somewhat eroded) for when you can and can't say something. And if they are wrong about something, they pay a price.

There are downsides to the *Free Press* to be sure. All of the things that make them reliable also make them risk averse and therefore slower than Internet pundits to both publish and to speculate on things. They are for-profit enterprises so they value sensation over substance although some norms work against this at places like the *New York Times* and the *Washington Post*. And yes, the average reporter at the established *Free Press* (not *Fox News* obviously) is to the left of the average American voter ideologically.

Despite these flaws, the *Free Press* (I'm partial to the *Times, Post, Atlantic, Wall Street Journal,* and a few others) are in my view the best source of facts. Therefore, I tend not to blog about facts until the *Free Press* has reported them (I will read other sources but not believe them or regurgitate them).

Analysis is something different though. Good analysis can come from anyone. And the Internet has allowed the sharing of good analysis far and wide. Twitter in particular is wonderful for this, but you have to manage your feed to both get good people and not be overwhelmed.

AUGUST 7, 2017: THE POLICIES OF WHITE RESENTMENT

Great article.[32] Money paragraph:

That white resentment simply found a new target for its ire is no coincidence; white identity is often defined by its sense of being ever under attack, with the system stacked against it. That's why Mr. Trump's policies are not aimed at ameliorating white resentment, but deepening it. His agenda is not, fundamentally, about creating jobs or protecting programs that benefit everyone, including whites; it's about creating purported enemies and then attacking them.

The million-dollar question is how many people are sufficiently attracted by the policies that hurt minorities that they ignore the policies that hurt everyone and the revelations of Trump's malfeasance still to come. If it's 25 percent of the electorate, Trump's presidency will be in danger soon. If it is 30 percent, he's right on the border. And if it is the vast majority of the current 35–37 percent that still approve of him, then we are in for a very dangerous three and a half years.

AUGUST 8, 2017: BAD NEWS AND GOOD NEWS FOR 2018 MIDTERMS

Bad news: David Wasserman has a depressing piece up on 538[33] discussing the inherent disadvantage that Democrats have in congressional elections. Money quote, "Even if Democrats were to win every single 2018 House and Senate race for seats representing places that Hillary Clinton won or

---

32 Carol Anderson, "The Politics of White Resentment," *New York Times*, August 5, 2017, https://www.nytimes.com/2017/08/05/opinion/sunday/white-resentment-affirmative-action.html.

33 David Wasserman, "The Congressional Map has a Record-Setting Bias Against Democrats," *FiveThirtyEight*, August 7, 2017, https://fivethirtyeight.com/features/the-congressional-map-is-historically-biased-toward-the-gop/.

that Trump won by less than 3 percentage points—a pretty good midterm by historical standards—they could still fall short of the House majority and lose five Senate seats." It's not all gerrymandering either (of course the Senate has nothing to do with gerrymandering).

Good news: Dems have opened up a ten-point lead in the generic congressional ballot. This is a very good predictor of midterm elections, even this far out. A ten-point win would flip the House easily.

Bad news: Republicans will continue to attempt to purge voter rolls as the story in the first comment below about Ohio shows. There is a big Supreme Court case in the fall on this subject.

Good news: Trump is the biggest asset the Democrats have right now. That could change, but every time he tweets or fires someone, a Democratic House candidate gains his wings.

Right now, I would say the Dems have about a 50 percent chance of taking back the House in 2018 and a 5 percent chance of taking back the Senate.

August 10, 2017: I feel about a nuclear attack on North Korea, the same way I feel about the erosion of our democratic system of governance. I am reasonably confident that there are sufficient safeguards in place to prevent it.

But two years ago, I thought both were impossible. The first and least likely step toward both was taken on November 8.

AUGUST 11, 2017: REMEMBER WHAT CANDIDATES SAY

On March 30, 2016, Chris Matthews told Trump that "nobody wants to hear a candidate for president talk about using nuclear weapons." Trump responded, "Then why are we making them?"

I still think that the US security apparatus and China will prevent the use of nuclear weapons in the current North Korea crisis. But in my view, the primary risk comes from Trump, not from Kim Jong Un. The head of North Korea knows that his use of a nuclear weapon means the end of his country. Trump does not face the same stakes. And he has a tremendous incentive to continue to escalate the crisis to take attention away from an investigation that is getting closer to him.

People complain all the time about the lies that candidates tell when they run for office. I've always paid far more attention to the far more frequent times when they truly speak their minds.

AUGUST 12, 2017: ANOTHER AWFUL NONSURPRISE

Yesterday I posted about how Trump's comments about nuclear weapons during the campaign presaged his comments provoking Kim Jong Un. Today is a repeat on the domestic front.

Today we have the neo-Nazi (I'm through calling them alt-right) demonstration in Virginia that lead to violence, one death, and the declaration of a state of emergency. During the campaign, Trump was hesitant to condemn David Duke, trafficked in anti-Semitic symbolism, and made outright racist remarks about immigrants and Muslims. He has a long history of racism toward African Americans.

So today's demonstration and violence should be no surprise. Trump has opened the scab on an American wound that never really healed. He made it OK to assert repugnant beliefs in public. He made it easier for the various strands of racism to connect and find each other. The violence today is an outgrowth of his hideous rhetoric in 2016...and many of us predicted it.

We fought for centuries to attach a stigma to racist actions. We are going to have to fight for years ahead to make sure that stigma reappears. Trump can "condemn the hate" all he wants but that is basically the arsonist condemning the fire.

AUGUST 15, 2017: CHARLOTTESVILLE

If your first reaction to the events of the past five days is anything besides revulsion at the behavior of Nazis and confederates in Chancellorsville (or hell, even at their very existence), then I have no interest in hearing your second or third reaction. You may want to talk about free speech. You may want to talk about the counter-protestors. But until you establish that you are aware that it was evil that was on the march, and that this country faces a crisis that involves first and foremost confronting that evil, shut the f&^% up. And that goes for the president as well.

AUGUST 17, 2017: REMEMBERING HISTORY AND SHADES OF GRAY

The neo-Nazis have equated the tearing down of statues of confederate generals with insulting Washington and Jefferson. Our neo-Nazi in chief picked up the theme in his tweets today.

To equate the confederate generals with the founders requires an impressive ignorance of history. A (very) brief (and vastly oversimplified) history lesson.

George Washington held slaves. He freed them upon his death. He led the Americans in the Revolutionary War that against all odds beat the British. He was the first president where he virtually invented the peaceful transition of power and set the American experiment on its way.

Thomas Jefferson held slaves and kept one as his mistress. He also wrote the Declaration of Independence (where he included a paragraph attacking slavery that had to be deleted to ensure southern support). He doubled the size of the United States as president. He also supported states' rights and a small federal government. A complicated legacy.

Robert E. Lee (to take the most sympathetic of the confederate generals) was an effective general and probably cared about those under his command. But in terms of public actions, he is known for one and one thing only: leading an army in rebellion against the United States to defend slavery.

As Josh Marshall pointed out in one of the articles[34] I posted yesterday, the statues of confederate generals got put up after Reconstruction to emphasize the re-subjugation of southern African Americans.

History is complicated. Some good people make morally atrocious choices. Some bad people are kind to their neighbors. But I know two things. Lee is worse than Jefferson and a lot worse than Washington. And Trump is the exception to the rule; he is all bad.

---

34 Josh Marshall, "Some Thoughts on Public Memory," *TPM*, August 14, 2017, http://talkingpointsmemo.com/edblog/some-thoughts-on-public-memory.

AUGUST 18, 2017: BANNON THEORIES

Since the Bannon news broke, I've heard the following theories:

- Bannon's firing will turn the neo-Nazis against Trump, as Breitbart leads the charge under Bannon's implicit or explicit guidance. Bannon may even talk to Mueller now.
- Kelly has asserted control over the White House, and, while he will never control Trump, this is a sign that leaks, and people from the inside undermining Trump will not be tolerated.
- Trump and Bannon coordinated this in order to spur further Charlottesville-like incidents and push us closer to civil unrest.

I don't know if any of these are true. Until we know more, speculation is just that, speculation. I will keep my take simple. A very dangerous person, no longer has an office in the West Wing of the White House. That is a good thing.

AUGUST 21, 2017: SYMPATHY FOR THE REPUBLICANS (*ROLLING STONES* REFERENCE INTENTIONAL)

One of the questions I hear the most often from progressives is "when will the Republicans finally realize Trump is a disaster and turn on him?" With Republican control of Congress and with congressional control of impeachment, this is a very relevant question. And those of us who have seen Trump as a unique threat are understandably impatient. But keep two things in mind.

1. The degree to which Republicans have already turned on Trump is unprecedented. It is unheard of seven months into a presidency to have members of your own party criticizing you publicly. And when was the last time you saw a Republican senator on a Sunday morning show defending Trump? Usually the president can count on members of Congress from his party to be his stalwart defenders and promoters. Trump can't.

2. In order for a Republican to turn on Trump, he or she has to make two sacrifices. They have to put their own reelection at risk (because of a potential primary from a Trump supporter—see Jeff Flake), and they have to be willing to hurt the chance that their own policy preferences will be enacted. Most representatives who are criticized for voting with Trump in Congress aren't doing it because they like Trump. They are doing it because they actually believe (as do many of their constituents) in Neil Gorsuch, in dismantling regulations, or in other conservative ideas. Undermining Trump hurts those priorities (yes, I agree many of those priorities are wrong-headed, and I'm not defending them). Democratic representatives face neither of these sacrifices.

That's why the failure of the health-care bill in the Senate was politically important. It lessened the second of these sacrifices. If Republicans aren't getting their policy preferences with Trump, why put up with him? And Charlottesville was important because all of a sudden, some Republicans have figured out that supporting Trump may hurt them as much as opposing him.

Yes, I believe Trump is unfit for office and dangerous (I think I've demonstrated that!). And I would like Republican elected officials to feel the same way. But I'm not surprised it is taking time for them to do so. When your representative finally says something bad about Trump, follow David Frum's advice, "Suggestion: if you want more people to quit the Trump train, the first react to a disembarkation should be 'Welcome' not 'Why not sooner?'"

AUGUST 22, 2017: A NORMAL AFGHANISTAN POLICY (MOSTLY)

NORMAL: Sending more troops to Afghanistan.

NORMAL: Saying you will use diplomacy to try and end our commitment there (even if you think it is NOT NORMAL).

NORMAL: Complaining about the situation your predecessors left you in.

NORMAL: Choosing a bad option when no option is good (they don't call Afghanistan "the graveyard of empires" for nothing).

The biggest NOT NORMAL piece is giving the military the unprecedented discretion that Trump has given it. Expect civilian casualties to rise.

The threat to Pakistan was also NOT NORMAL, but let's see what is actually done before panicking.

AUGUST 23, 2017: SCENARIO 2?

In my cataloging of possible ways that the Trump presidency would end, scenario 2 was a sudden end where he leaves office in response to some event. Keith Olbermann yesterday predicted that this would happen soon[35] with a Trump resignation as Mueller's investigation closes in on some (unknown) big reveal.

I'm not exactly clear on Trump's motive to resign. Let's game this out.

1. Trump is guilty of something yooge, and he knows it. Then the presidency protects him from prosecution. He only resigns, if he is promised a pardon from soon to be President Pence (probably for his kids too). Plausible, but one glaring problem. Rumor has it that New York AG Eric Schneiderman is investigating Trump for financial misdeeds. These would be state crimes, and Trump could not be pardoned for them by the president. Why accept a pardon deal, if you are still at risk of prosecution?

2. Trump is guilty of something but either doesn't realize it or is too arrogant to think he'll get caught. No way, he resigns in this scenario.

3. Trump is innocent (suppressing laughter) and sick of being president and feeling persecuted. He wants to go make money. Trump

---

35 Rebecca Shapiro, "Keith Olbermann Predicts how it Will All End for Trump," *Huffington Post*, August 23, 2017, http://www.huffingtonpost.com/entry/keith-olbermann-trump-end-resign_us_599d0b73e4b0a296083ae352.

does have a history of giving up on things when they turn sour so maybe. But he's not innocent so this isn't really relevant.

In short, I see the resignation soon as pretty implausible, but not impossible. On the other hand, September is going to be ugly (debt-ceiling debate and budget showdown over the wall in Congress). His relationship with Republicans in Congress is at an all-time low (see article on McConnell-Trump feud in the first comment). He gave another unhinged speech in Arizona last night (see crazy list of things in the second comment) that will do nothing for his approval ratings (still falling gradually). If a resignation were coming, the timing would make sense. I just don't think it's coming.

AUGUST 25, 2017: DON'T FORGET RUSSIA

With so much going on the world of white supremacy and Republican infighting, it is easy to forget about the scandal that is most likely to bring this presidency down. In the past week:

- It was reported that Trump complained to three GOP senators about the Russia probe. It's clear he hasn't forgotten about it.
- We saw revelations that yet another member of the Trump campaign tried to set up meetings with Russia (this time a former Sessions chief of staff).
- The man who commissioned the Steele Dossier testified for hours before the Senate Judiciary Committee and reportedly turned over reams of documents.

This won't go away. As it progresses keep in mind why it is happening. The following four facts are relatively undisputed.

1. Russians hacked the DNC and worked to reveal the e-mails at times harmful to Clinton.
2. A crazy number of high-ranking officials in the Trump campaign had ties to Russia. The candidate's son met with Russian operatives.

3. Michael Flynn talked with Russia before the inauguration about plans to eliminate sanctions.
4. Trump fired Comey for investigating the above.

To me these four facts make it very likely that Trump is guilty of obstruction of justice and possibly of much more. Mueller has been plugging away quietly on his investigation. But just because he's been quiet doesn't mean that it is going away.

AUGUST 25, 2017: SO TONIGHT

- A category 4 hurricane is bearing down on Texas.
- North Korea fired missiles.
- Trump pardoned racist Sheriff Joe Arpaio.
- Gorka resigned from the White House.
- News broke that Mueller had issued subpoenas to Manafort associated and is investigating Flynn's role in the e-mail scandal.
- Trump issued his transgender order to DOD.

As someone said on Twitter, this is the type of night they train you for in chryon school.

AUGUST 27, 2017: TRUMP AND "BIG GOVERNMENT" (ORIGINALLY APPEARED IN THE *HILL*)[36]

The Republican Party has long touted itself as the party of limited government. In this sense, Donald Trump was always a different kind of Republican candidate. He ran as a populist rather than a conservative, and many of his proposals, if successfully implemented, would have made the reach of government larger, not smaller.

---

36 Stuart Shapiro, "In the Era of Trump, Big Government is Winning," *The Hill*, August 26, 2017, http://thehill.com/blogs/pundits-blog/the-administration/348109-in-the-era-of-trump-big-government-is-winning#bottom-story-socials.

As president, Trump has continued to champion initiatives on both sides of the big government or small government divide. But, perhaps not surprisingly, his rate of success has been very different in expanding government than it has been in contracting it.

Just this week, President Trump announced the expansion of our military role in Afghanistan. This is consistent with his proposed budget expanding military spending, one of the few parts of his budget that has been positively received by Congress (in fact Congress has argued that the spending increase for the Department of Defense was not enough).

The most successful member of Trump's cabinet in enacting policy changes has been Attorney General Jeff Sessions. Sessions has increased the reach of government by creating a new asset forfeiture policy, cracking down on marijuana law enforcement, and pushing for stricter sentencing.

The other signature area in which Trump has been most successful is immigration. Increased action by the Immigration and Customs Enforcement (ICE) has been an explicit goal of the Trump administrations, and deportations and arrests have increased. Stories of the impact on communities of having valued members removed have become common.

Contrast this with Trump's efforts to roll back Obamacare, which met with a dramatic failure in the Senate. While the ultimate fate of Affordable Care Act is not certain, the likelihood that the signature legislation of the Obama administration will survive in some form is much greater than it was several months ago.

In the regulatory arena, Trump's attempts to repeal and delay regulations have begun to run up against predictable legal obstacles. The repeals will take years to implement and may be overturned by courts. Courts have also made clear that attempts to delay Obama administration regulations cannot be used indefinitely and that eventually the Trump administration must either implement these regulations or engage in the uncertain prospects of repealing them.

Finally, in September, Congress will have to pass a budget for fiscal year 2018 (or more likely a continuing resolution until they can agree on a permanent budget). While the Trump administration has proposed draconian cuts, even Republicans have acknowledged that these reductions have no chance of passing. Some agencies will face funding losses, but they are far more likely to be incremental than draconian.

Trump's most successful attempts to reduce the role of government have largely been accomplished by appointing unqualified people to head federal agencies. At the Department of Housing and Urban Development, Secretary Ben Carson's management has led qualified career employees to begin to give up hope in the agency. At the Department of Energy, Secretary Rick Perry's oversight has led to questions about the oversight of our nuclear arsenal. Even the most committed small government activists have to question this style of downsizing.

Why has Trump ended up being a big government president in his first year in office? I suspect it is for two reasons. The first is that dismantling government programs is harder than creating them. The second is that Trump cares more about expanding the police powers of the government than he does about reducing the overall role of government.

Libertarians were among the most reluctant Republican supporters of Trump's campaign. The expansion of government as a police state and the failure of it to downsize elsewhere is proving them prophetic.

AUGUST 29, 2017: TRUMP AND THE REPUBLICANS

In the past few weeks, Trump has attacked Republican Senators Flake and Corker and has engaged in open warfare with Majority Leader McConnell. Meanwhile, more Republicans have started to condemn the president (particularly his response to Charlottesville and the pardon of Arpaio). John Kasich has made very real sounds about challenging Trump in 2020.

Putting aside the issue of whether we are still a republic in 2020, it's not gonna work out that simply for Republicans. The Republican Party is Trump's party now. For years after the Civil Rights Act passed, they put into action Richard Nixon's southern strategy. They appealed to white voters, talked about crime and drugs as code words for African Americans, and they lost the legacy of Lincoln that they so often trumpeted.

Trump is the logical conclusion of this process. His ascendance was abated by the election of the first African American president, and by a weird primary with sixteen candidates, but regardless of how it happened, he did win. And in doing so, he has completed the process that Nixon started a generation earlier. His loyalists are very loyal. They won't quickly forget a GOP establishment that either betrays Trump through impeachment or does not sufficiently support him. And they make up a majority of the Republican Party. The GOP won't be able to go back to nominating Bushes and telling the Trump base that everything will work out OK.

So now Republicanism means Trumpism. What that means for conservativism (Trump is most certainly not a conservative) in America is an open question. What that means for individual conservatives like Sasse and Flake will be up to them. Either they live up to their words and leave the party or fall in line behind their party's new dear leader.

AUGUST 30, 2017: I BEG YOUR PARDON

Last week President Trump pardoned Sheriff Joe Arpaio. The pardon was appalling; a further assertion of Trump's disregard for norms and for the rights of Hispanics that Arpaio trampled on. It was not unconstitutional, however. The presidential pardon power is relatively unlimited in the constitution.

Many have speculated that the pardon was a bit of a test by Trump. How will the public and Congress react when Trump pardons those caught up in the Russia investigation: Paul Manafort (who seems close to being indicted), Michael Flynn (ditto), Jared Kushner, Donald Trump Jr. himself?

The article below[37] contains the responses of ten legal experts to what will happen if Trump tries to pardon those who may implicate him in Russiagate. While the headline is optimistic, the answers themselves are more modest.

Basically, once Trump pardons Manafort et al. (and I have no doubt these pardons are coming), they can no longer claim the fifth amendment and refuse to testify on Russia (because they face no risk of prosecution). So they will be free to confess their roles. But they could lie. Then if

---

37 Sean Illing, "Ten Legal Experts on Why Trump Can't Pardon his Way out of the Russia Investigation," *Vox.com*, August 27, 2017, https://www.vox.com/2017/8/29/16211784/donald-trump-pardon-constitution-michael-flynn-manafort.

they are prosecuted for perjury, Trump could pardon them for that. Or they could refuse to testify and be prosecuted for contempt of court (or Congress). Trump could pardon them for that.

But each pardon has a political cost. Arpaio's pardon has not helped Trump among the general public (and may have hurt), but his base liked it. We can assume that every pardon further will act the same way.

Matt Glassman (a great follow on Twitter) predicted back in March that the constitutional crisis that would define this presidency would begin with a pardon. It will be relatively soon I think. And the resolution of that crisis will depend on politics. If the public reacts to pardons by calling their representative (particularly their Republican ones) and calling for impeachment and by forcing Trump's poll numbers down further, then the pardons will be the beginning of the end for him. If they don't, it could be the beginning of the end for the rest of us.

SEPTEMBER 1: A LONG SEPTEMBER?

Amid the nearly constant Mueller revelations, the hurricane, and the tweet that is always around the corner, Congress returns on Tuesday. And they have a lot to do in a month. As Matt Glassman notes,[38] there are three pieces of "must pass legislation."

- Raising the debt ceiling
- A continuing resolution to keep the government open while a final budget is negotiated
- Several reauthorizations of popular programs

Oddly the hurricane may have helped here as there will likely be a fourth piece of must-pass legislation, Harvey relief. Money for the hurricane will be hard to veto and to vote against, particularly if you are from Texas. If it is attached to any of the above pieces of legislation, the combined bill will win over some of the opponents fearful of being portrayed as voting

---

38 Matt Glassman "A Hard Rain's Gonna Fall," *Five Points* September 1, 2017, https://tinyletter.com/MattGlassman/letters/five-points-a-hard-rain-s-gonna-fall.

against hurricane relief. In fact any number of these bills could get combined together.

But there are no guarantees. A clever rider (like one protecting the Dreamers or on the opposite side, something to do with the wall) could make the debate much more contentious. And this Congress seems incapable of doing anything the easy way.

(Note: Behind these bills comes tax reform and a final budget [bills guaranteed to be controversial], so congressional leadership has an incentive to finish things quickly).

SEPTEMBER 3, 2017

This article[39] has been making its way around the Internet. It is one of the most thorough dissections of "Why Trump" and places Trump in a historical and comparative context. I highly recommend it. That said, it is twenty-five single-spaced pages so leave some time.

It basically argues that Trump is the product of three simultaneous phenomena.

1. High levels of partisanship and an increasingly powerful presidency
2. The sorting of parties by race combined with inequality, which has a high racial component
3. The erosion of democratic norms

There is much, much more to it than that, and these phenomena overlap considerably. Their conclusion is not cheery:

We can conclude with three observations about the contemporary moment in American politics. First, is American democracy under threat? Our answer is yes: comparative experience suggests that

---

39 Lieberman, Robert C., Suzanne Mettler, Thomas B. Pepinsky, Kenneth M. Roberts, and Richard Valelly. "Trumpism and American Democracy: History, Comparison, and the Predicament of Liberal Democracy in the United States." (2017). https://papers.ssrn.com/sol3/papers.cfm?abstract_id=3028990.

these are not propitious conditions for democratic durability, and certainly not for effective government performance. How serious is the threat? It is hard to argue that contemporary American democracy faces a more acute threat than it did during the Civil War. But once-unthinkable scenarios now seem plausible: an unconstitutional third term in office, for example, or emergency government in the wake of a terrorist attack. Or we may see truly systematic disenfranchisement of American voters. It is the multi-faceted nature of our moment that is so distinctive and worrisome.

Second, our framework considers institutions, the boundaries of civic membership and status, and norms as bearing an interactive relationship to one another. The sorting of parties in a racialized polity has enabled a certain type of exclusionary candidacy in a far more presidential regime. This kind of interactive complexity raises the stakes for democratic stability, for it enables the corrosion of norms of executive restraint, with possibly broader repercussions for campaign strategy and voter mobilization around exclusionary white nationalist motifs.

Finally, politics will matter, spanning all three of our dimensions, in ways that are hard to predict. The defense of norms and institutions of inclusive citizenship will be exceptionally important as we go forward, for example, as will debates about how to address the corrosive effects of rising inequality. Indeed, all of the norms and institutions that we discussed will require defense and renewal. The very scope of the challenge underscores the gravity of the current moment—and the need to be open to lessons from other national and political histories that once seemed of little relevance to the American experience.

SEPTEMBER 5, 2017: TURNING DREAMS INTO NIGHTMARES

The upcoming decision by Trump on the fate of the beneficiaries of President Obama's Deferred Action for Childhood Arrivals (a.k.a. "The Dreamers") has taken over the headlines. Rumor has it that President Trump will announce that the Dreamers will no longer enjoy special protections after six months pass unless Congress passes a statute to help them.

This article[40] is the best summary I've seen on the implications of the possible Trump decision. Some points that have been underemphasized in the media are as follows:

- If Trump had not acted, the courts likely would have done the same thing.
- That doesn't mean that Trump could not have come up with better responses to the pending lawsuit from the states (including trying to fight it while prodding Congress to act).
- State lawsuits protecting the dreamers are unlikely to be successful.
- The Dreamers will return to their pre-2012 status. They won't be rounded up and deported, but their ability to work will be drastically reduced. And they will have to constantly look over their shoulders.
- Congress still has the power to protect them and with must-pass legislation coming up in September (see post last week), a brave legislator can try and attach the Dream Act to one of those bills. I'm not terribly confident it will happen, but it is possible.

None of this is to minimize Trump's action (or potential action, it hasn't actually been announced yet). While legal, it is immoral. It is of a piece with the Charlottesville response and the Arpaio pardon. All are the actions of a president who cares only about one constituency—those who most ardently support him—and not someone who is the president of the entire country.

---

40 Eric Columbus, "If Trump Ends DACA, What Happens to the Dreamers?" *Politico*, August 31, 2017, http://www.politico.com/magazine/story/2017/08/31/daca-dreamers-donald-trump-215564.

SEPTEMBER 6, 2017: HURRICANE DONALD MAKES LANDFALL

Trump has done lots of bad things, particularly when it comes to immigration. But many of his wholesale policy changes have failed. We still have Obamacare. Trump's immigration EOs are tied up in the courts. The number of regulations he has thus far repealed is vanishingly small.

Until yesterday, Trump's worst actions have been less tangible. He has given white supremacists a more powerful voice, not only in government (which was bad enough) but in society at large. He has given comfort to repressive leaders around the world and in doing so put dissidents in Turkey, Saudi Arabia, and the Philippines at greater risk. He has increased the risk of armed conflict. He has enhanced China's position in the world. He has eroded faith both in America's ideals and its competence.

The scheduled end of DACA is different. It affects people immediately. Even though the dreamers don't face the loss of their rights immediately, they must immediately begin planning as if they do. If I were advising them, I would say, "Don't travel, change your cell phone number, and save your money." As someone who has never been told those things, I find it hard to imagine what it must feel like to hear them.

The best chance to save the dreamers comes in the next month as Congress crafts "must pass" legislation on the debt ceiling, the budget, and Harvey recovery (and perhaps Irma recovery). I think the Democrats have done a wonderful job thus far opposing Trump. But this is a bigger test. They should hold up this legislation until protection for the dreamers is included. The dreamers need relief in the same sense that victims of Harvey do. Tell your representative this.

SEPTEMBER 7, 2017: THE ART (?) OF THE DEAL

I'm pretty flummoxed by yesterday's deal between Trump, Pelosi, and Schumer. In case you missed it, Trump, to the consternation of McConnell and Ryan, agreed to a package that includes a three-month extension of the debt ceiling, a three-month budget resolution, and Harvey relief funding. Here's how I see it from the perspective of the players.

Trump: He may have made his mind up on the spot (as he often does). But I think he is a winner here. After a good hurricane response, now he can say he is a deal maker. Also, Trump knows his voters better than the Republicans; they don't care about the debt ceiling or spending. Ugh, this is the main reason I don't like the deal; it helps Trump.

Pelosi-Schumer: They must think that the chance of helping the Dreamers will be better in December than now. I'm not sure why that is true. But they may know something I don't, many people do.

McConnell-Ryan: As Kevin Drum notes[41], they may be crying crocodile tears over this. Their big problem was going to be their right flank, not the Democrats. This neuters them for three months. Although it does just postpone the problem.

The Freedom Caucus: OK, here is a reason to be happy about the deal: they don't like it, and I think their misery (unlike Ryan-McConnell) is likely genuine.

We won't really be able to evaluate the deal until its successor happens in December. And as the past three months have taught us, a lot can happen between now and then.

SEPTEMBER 10, 2017: THE PERFECT TIME TO TALK ABOUT CLIMATE CHANGE

Scott Pruitt said that while hurricanes were bearing down on the southern United States, it was not the right time to talk about climate change. While the comment set the Twitterverse going ("Scott Pruitt just got diagnosed with diabetes, but it's the wrong time to talk about sugar"; "Scott Pruitt as captain of the *Titanic*; it's the wrong time to talk about icebergs."), his statement highlights a serious problem for the reality-based community.

Scientists will always say that a particular storm cannot be attributed to climate change, which is absolutely right. Scientists like to be precise and to be accurate, and this gives them a serious disadvantage in political debates.

---

41 Kevin Drum, "OK I Guess Ryan and McConnell Really Did Get Taken to the Cleaners," *Mother Jones*, September 7, 2017, http://www.motherjones.com/kevin-drum/2017/09/ok-i-guess-ryan-and-mcconnell-really-did-get-taken-to-the-cleaners/

When there is a storm like this, scientists say, "Don't attribute it to climate change," and climate mystics like Pruitt say, "It's not a good time." When there is a cool summer day or a snowstorm, scientists say, "That doesn't prove anything," and climate mystics like Senator James Inhofe throw snowballs on the floor of the Senate. Is there any surprise, we are losing here?

Now I don't want scientists to lie. But whenever there is a storm like Harvey and Irma, those of us who understand the scientific consensus on climate change need to be out front saying, climate change makes storms like Harvey and Irma more likely. It makes them more severe. And if we don't stop it, these storms are going to be looked at as quaint from the perspective of the late twenty-first century. And the next time there is a snowstorm, tell people to take pictures and enjoy it so they can tell their grandkids what they were like. Is that so hard?

SEPTEMBER 11, 2017: TRUMP AND THE REPUBLICANS (REDUX)

The *Times* this weekend published a very silly article about how Trump's deal with Pelosi and Schumer may signal that he is more an independent than a Republican, and that he is a threat to the two-party system.

Critics rightly pointed out that his policies on a wide range of issues such as immigration, Obamacare, climate change, and so on have been Republican orthodoxy so one deal doesn't change any of that. I want to focus on another problem with the *Times'* argument.

Trump now *is* the Republican Party. The reason he could make the deal last week is that Republican voters have never cared as much about "small government" as their leaders have. The voters went along with it, particularly since coded language convinced them that big government meant their tax dollars going to immigrants and minorities, but they don't really want to see government benefits go away, even for a short time.

No, unless Paul Ryan and the Tea Partiers abandon their small government philosophy, it is they who don't have a home in the Republican Party any more. The party now stands for Trumpism, and Ryan et al. now have three choices. They can admit the whole small government thing was a fake and get on board. They can leave the party and form a third party (or join the libertarians). Or they can fight what will likely be a losing battle to get control back. Which course they take will have a lot to do with how national politics plays out over the next decade.

While I am hopeful (though still not convinced) that the country can survive Trump, it is not clear to me that the Republican Party (as we've known it since Nixon) can. And in that sense, the *Times* article was right, but not for the reasons it gave.

SEPTEMBER 13, 2017: THE BOOK

Yesterday, Hillary Clinton's book came out, and the Internet exploded. I have two simple observations, and then (I hope) I will stay away from this train wreck of a subject.

- Hillary Clinton has every right to write this book, and wishes that she would "just go away" are obnoxious and—unless you are saying that about *every* other failed presidential candidate—sexist. Hillary won more votes for president than anyone not named Obama. She has an audience who wants to hear from her, and she deserves to tell her side of the story.
- I've read excerpts online of the book (I have no intention of buying it). I agree with much of what she says in her analysis of the 2016 election but do disagree with some of her points.

I realize this is fairly banal, but it wouldn't surprise me if even these statements offend large groups of people. Such is the radioactive cloud that surrounds Hillary.

SEPTEMBER 15, 2017: THE PERMANENCE OF OBAMA

I like the analysis below[42] because it says what I've been saying numerous contexts for the past eight months. For all the rhetoric and for all the angst

---

42 Perry Bacon Jr., "Trump Hasn't Dismantled Obama's Legacy Yet—And May Not Ever," *Fivethirtyeight*, September 14, 2017. https://fivethirtyeight.com/features/obama-v-trump/.

on the left, much of President Obama's record is intact and will remain so. The biggest threat was to the Affordable Care Act and by one vote in the Senate, it hung on (although there are rumors that the GOP will take one more swing at it this month).

The parts of Obama's legacy that were most vulnerable were always going to be those things he accomplished with the pen and the phone. That's why the DACA recipients are in trouble and why Sessions has been so successful at DOJ.

But as for the laws that were passed and the regulations that were issued, 99 percent of them are going to stay in place. And that legacy (coupled with Obama's status as the first African American president and the Iran deal and the opening of Cuba and…) will result in Obama being seen as a top-ten president, no matter what Trump does.

SEPTEMBER 18, 2017: REMEMBER NOT NORMAL IS NOT NORMAL

In the past week, you may not have noticed:

Trump met with Senator Tim Scott, the only Black Republican in Congress, to discuss why Trump's actions after Charlottesville were so awful. Scott emerged from the meeting talking about how Trump was willing to listen. A day later Trump summarized the meeting by highlighting how right his Charlottesville reaction was, "I think, especially in light of the advent of Antifa, if you look at what's going on there, you have some pretty bad dudes on the other side also, and essentially that's what I said." NOT NORMAL

This weekend, Trump retweeted a gif of him hitting Secretary Clinton with a golf ball. While the tweet itself deservedly got a lot of attention, less attention was given to the fact that the original tweeter had previously tweeted anti-Semitic material. NOT NORMAL

I grow increasingly alarmed at how successfully Trump has driven down the level of discourse. Either of the above would have been front page news a year (or even six months) ago. But we now take for granted that our commander in chief is a white supremacist (well except when an African American female ESPN host says so). Once that is normalized, what comes next?

SEPTEMBER 19, 2017: IT'S BACK

Much like the *Terminator*, the effort to repeal Obamacare won't die. Also much like the *Terminator*, those behind the effort won't be happy until thousands of people are dead.

The vehicle this time is the Graham-Cassidy bill in the Senate, which is essentially a gutting of Medicaid and a transfer of funds from states that have expanded Medicaid to those that haven't (from blue states to red, who would have thought).

Proponents of the bill claim they have forty-nine yes votes. Remember that they need fifty to pass it. There are two asterisks though. One is that forty-nine senators have not yet come out publicly for the bill so it is possible that Senator Graham is bluffing. The second is that they *must* pass the bill by September 30 or else they will need an impossible sixty votes to pass it.

The drill over the next few weeks will be painfully familiar. A rushed CBO score, constricted debate in the Senate (even more constricted than in July because time is shorter), and maybe a vote.

My read of the situation is that there are at least twenty GOP senators who want this bill to fail but only a few who may have the courage to join Senators Collins and Murkowski and be the ones to kill it. If I had to bet, I'd wager it won't come up for a vote. But I wouldn't want to bet on the lives of the least fortunate. Instead I'd call my senators, especially if I lived in Maine (Collins), Alaska (Murkowski), Arizona (McCain), West Virginia (Capito), and Ohio (Portman).

SEPTEMBER 21, 2017: ME FIRST

In the past few days,

- Trump has given a terrifying speech at the UN about how he was going to take care of America First (a slogan first popularized by Nazi sympathizer Charles Lindbergh and hardly appropriate for the *United* Nations).
- It was revealed that HHS Secretary Tom Price who criticized the use of private jets by government officials when he was in Congress

took five chartered flights last week at a cost of tens of thousands of dollars more than commercial travel.

- White House economic adviser Stephen Moore said that "people want insurance for their own families, not other people's."

Notice a pattern here? The consistent mentality throughout the Trump administration is selfishness to the extreme. Selfishness in personal behavior and selfishness as a guiding principle for public policy.

Now I'm OK with some self-interested behavior, particularly in private transactions. But a huge part of the role of government is ensuring that this self-interested behavior is curbed before it hurts other people. Another big part is ensuring that we are a community within this country and that our country is part of a larger global community.

There is so much that bothers me about the Trump administration. But this consistent devotion to selfishness as an organizing principle for society is up near the top.

There is one consolation. If or when Mueller starts taking this gang down, it will clearly be everyone for themselves, which will make it easier.

SEPTEMBER 22, 2017: THE WEEK IN TRUMP-RUSSIA

This article[43] gives a great summary of the revelations this week in Mueller's investigation of Trump. It's been a bad week to be Paul Manafort and therefore probably a bad week for Trump. It looks a lot like Manafort is going down. It also looks like Trump may abandon him (at least publicly).

Not in the article is the fact that Trump's approval rating is back up over thirty-nine. Regardless of what is going on in the investigation, this gives Trump some protection for a while. But Trump is his own worst enemy, and a Mueller indictment of Manafort is unlikely to be handled by Trump in a quiet confident manner.

---

43 David A. Graham, "The Paradox of an Explosive Week in the Mueller Investigation," *The Atlantic*, September 21, 2017, https://www.theatlantic.com/politics/archive/2017/09/muellers-probe-of-many-colors/540570/.

SEPTEMBER 23, 2017: FIRE THAT SON OF A B^&@H

The title of this post seemingly refers to President Trump's comments about national anthem protesters in professional football (most prominently Colin Kaepernick) yesterday.

Many have noted that Trump used harsher language about Kaepernick than he did about the white nationalists in Charlottesville ("some of them are good people"). It shows both his racial attitudes and his attitude toward dissent. He watches in envy as Erdogan's bodyguards beat up protesters.

Nah, the title of this post refers toward my attitude about this least American of presidents.

SEPTEMBER 25, 2017: SPORTS AND POLITICS

When Adolf Hitler proclaimed that German athletes were superior to all others, that was politics.

When we cheered Joe Louis and Jesse Owens proving him wrong, that was politics.

When Muhammad Ali did not go to Vietnam, that was politics.

When he was stripped of his heavyweight title, that was politics.

When it was decided that the national anthem and *God Bless America* would be played at sporting events, that was politics.

When Colin Kaepernick kneeled to protest police brutality, that was politics.

Two points:

Sports, because it looms so large in our society, has always been mixed with politics.

And you can't ask to keep politics out of sports when you don't like the underlying cause but ignore the political relationship when you do like it.

(Oh, one more point, Lebron James and Stephen Curry are awesome.)

SEPTEMBER 26, 2017: AMATEUR HOUR

Eric Garland has been off his game for a while, but he absolutely nails it with this tweetstorm.[44] This past week more than any other has shown the

---

44 See tweetstorm at: https://twitter.com/ericgarland/status/91244920048818177.

cost of having a president who doesn't know the first think about government. Apart from his white-supremacist attitudes, his lack of competence is the worst aspect of his presidency. He has us in a situation where the following has resulted:

- Puerto Rico is without power, and no government help is on the way (apparently an aid package will go to Congress in a week).
- The risk of a nuclear showdown is higher than it has been since the Cold War.
- A new travel ban has been issued that is much like the one in January but with a pretty bow on it. It is most likely illegal, but it will hurt those who are trying to come here because they believed in the idea of America.
- Regardless of what happens with Graham-Cassidy, HHS will continue to undermine Obamacare.

None of this would be happening with President Clinton. None of it would be happening with President Sanders. None of it (except maybe the last one but I doubt it) would be happening with President Bush or President Rubio. And as Garland points out, for that I will never forgive Trump supporters.

SEPTEMBER 27, 2017: THE SENATE GETS LESS STRANGE BUT MOORE CRAZY

Both Trump and (especially) Senator McConnell had a very bad day yesterday.

- In Alabama, Roy Moore won the Senate Republican primary despite Trump endorsing and McConnell financing his opponent, Luther Strange. Moore was removed from his position as Alabama Chief Justice, not once but twice. The first time was for refusing to remove a statue of the ten commandments in his courtroom. He was also later suspended (after being elected back as chief justice— you have to love Alabama) for refusing to enforce the Supreme Court's gay marriage ruling.

- Obamacare repeal died again. McConnell somehow thought this time would be different, and Trump again fails to deliver on one of his signature campaign promises.

It is nice to see both Trump and McConnell suffer, but it's hard to be too happy about Roy Moore as a US senator (so donate to his Democratic opponent). He's gonna make Ted Cruz look good.

SEPTEMBER 29, 2017: THE LIES

You often hear that all politicians lie. And in the narrowest sense, that is true. But few of them make a habit of it, and most keep their promises (one study said that 70 percent of promises that recent presidents made on the campaign trail were upheld).

Trump's lying is different. It is NOT NORMAL. On Twitter, this week he claimed that the Obamacare repeal failed because one Republican senator was in the hospital. This is demonstrably untrue. And it is an utterly unnecessary lie, Trump could have (and has) spun a story about how it failed because McConnell failed or because Dems stood united against it. Why add this lie?

For his tax reform, the lies have been coming fast and furious. I'm not talking about the "tax cuts will spur growth and therefore be revenue neutral" argument. I think this is empirically invalid, but the argument has been around long enough that I can't fault Trump (in particular) for using it. No, I'm talking about things like "rich people will pay more" and "I won't benefit from this." These are again statements that are easy to disprove and utterly unnecessary for his side of the debate.

I'm not about to psychoanalyze Trump. Frankly, I don't care why his lying is pathological. What I do care about is its impact. It is (like his white nationalism and his love of foreign dictators) corroding the body politic. Politicians who rarely lied before will do so more frequently. Their constituents will expect it and shrug at it. When a politician does get caught in a lie, Trump supporters will draw equivalencies to Trump. The truth is another long-term casualty of this disastrous presidency.

SEPTEMBER 30, 2017: ACTING NORMAL IN THE FACE OF NOT NORMAL

I was at an event in DC yesterday. Attendees were government employees and academics. People from across the ideological spectrum, all of whom I have a great deal of respect for.

The thing that struck me though was how normal everyone behaved. National policy issues were discussed as if we were in the presence of a NORMAL presidency. Perhaps stress levels were a bit higher (I couldn't tell) but nothing at the existential level to be sure.

On the one hand, this is reassuring. It reflects a tacit belief that this too will pass. That the system will withstand Trump, and the country and world will go on, perhaps much as it did before. Certainly most of the people in the room were people who would think about these things, and perhaps they have reached the conclusion eventually that he will be gone and we will go back to discussing and arguing about health care and other subjects not Trump related.

But it was also disconcerting. What if they are wrong? Surely elites in Turkey saw Erdogan as something that would pass and went about their lives and their work a dozen years ago. Would more panic now help or would it simply be stress that would do little to prevent whatever is coming next? I guess I've struggled with this myself as the months tick by. Probably many of you have as well.

Well I'll keep panicking and spewing forth because my gut tells me pretty clearly that the dangers are real. But I will hope that I am wrong. Better stressed than sorry.

OCTOBER 2, 2017

I gave up on gun control at the federal level after Sandy Hook. So my hope in the wake of the horrible news from Las Vegas is that we start calling events like this "terrorist attacks," since that's what they are. Then maybe we can realize that when some sicko kills a bunch of people, it matters less why they did it (or what nationality or religion they are) than that they did it. Maybe in the long run that will make a difference.

OCTOBER 3, 2017: THE POLITICS OF GUN CONTROL

Look, I hate the NRA as much as anyone. But the gut reaction to yesterday of saying Congress is bought and paid for by the NRA is misguided. Roughly half of Congress comes from states or districts where they represent a *public* that vehemently opposes most gun control measures. And yes, while polls show that some smaller reasonable measures command a majority of support, all indications are that this support is thin.

In other words let's say a high-capacity magazine ban comes up before Congress. The representatives from that half of the country that oppose gun control face the following dilemma. The measure polls favorably in their district (let's say 70–30). But that 30 percent that are opposed will never again support their representative if he votes for it. The 70 percent in favor contain quite a few people who will forgive the representative for voting against it (because they are generally against gun control). The rational (not the moral of course) move is to vote against the measure.

So when we say we want gun control to pass, the solution isn't to complain about the NRA. They may make the situation worse, but I suspect they do far more to profit and exploit existing preferences than to create them. The solution is to change hearts and minds. And when I said yesterday I gave up after Sandy Hook, that's because if that didn't that change hearts and minds, nothing will.

State and local laws are more likely to change and will make a difference. So I'd recommend focusing energy there.

One last thought. Gun control has its origins in part in southern white efforts to keep guns out of the hands of African Americans. The ironies abound, but it wouldn't surprise me if the reactions to a black person killing sixty people differed from when a white person does it (sadly, a Muslim wouldn't do the trick, the response would be call for a stronger travel ban).

OCTOBER 5, 2017: ONE LITTLE PLEASURE

Regular readers know there is not much I enjoy about the Trump Administration but I must admit there is one thing that has consistently made me happy.

When Trump humiliates someone who works for his administration, an angel gets their wings. First it was Sessions getting screamed at for recusing himself from the Russia investigation. Then Price last week had to be yelled at for two hours before he got fired. And then this weekend was the latest episode of let's embarrass Rex Tillerson publicly as Trump undermined his trip to Asia on Twitter (and we now know what Tillerson thinks of Trump meaning there is more of this coming).

These guys all bought in to working for Trump thinking they'd be able to weather it and that they were set for life. They could use Trump they thought. Now they are being made fools of in what will hopefully be the last job for most of them. Couldn't happen to a better bunch of guys.

OCTOBER 6, 2017

Big news day yesterday. What stood out was the news that Mueller and Steele (of Steele Dossier fame) have spoken even though Steele has not met with Senate Intelligence Committee. There are two major implications of this.

- Mueller takes the Steele dossier seriously. This doesn't mean every detail in it is correct (pee pee!) but even if half of it is correct, Trump and his campaign are guilty of some pretty bad stuff.
- Either Mueller or Steele really does not trust the Senate committee (there is now news that Steele will meet with them, but this was probably held off until Mueller had secured his information).

Perhaps Trump's very odd comment that this was the "calm before the storm" comment was related to this. Perhaps it was related to something else (North Korea?). Perhaps it was just something he said (covfefe?). But there is a storm coming, not clear how soon but it's coming.

OCTOBER 8, 2017: PARTING THE WATERS

I recently finished reading Taylor Branch's nine-hundred-page *Parting the Waters: America in the King Years 1954–1963* (it took me three months).

One of the best history books I've read. Here is the review I wrote on Amazon:

This book chronicles the civil rights movement from 1954 to 1963. It is a stunningly well-researched, well-written, and educational piece of work. I cannot wait to read the two sequels that take the reader up through Martin Luther King's death.

King is, of course, the focus of the book and obviously justifiably so. He is three dimensional, and his faults as a leader of the movement are presented as carefully as his strengths. And one gets a clear sense of his growth as a leader over the nine years covered.

For me though, the highlight was reading about the many other heroes who played a role in the civil rights movement. From Robert Moses organizing voting drives in Mississippi to John Doar, a white midwestern lawyer who finds himself at the Department of Justice, to preachers like Ralph Abernathy and Fred Shuttlesworth. These were names I did not know before reading the book and now will not forget.

The book shies away from King's personal life (Coretta fades almost entirely to the background after marrying King) and does not cover strands of the movement such as the one led by Malcolm X. Clocking in at 920 pages, one can't criticize the book for leaving things out though. Branch chose his lens for the work and applied it expertly.

OCTOBER 9, 2017: NOISE AND NEWS

In a weekend with more super annoying stories (and one or two real ones) than any in a long time, I've decided to treat the weekend with the seriousness it deserves.

Winner of the weekend: Senator Corker of Tennessee both for his nursing home comment and his clear attempt to embarrass his colleagues into coming out against Trump.

Whiners of the weekend: All the people who complained that Corker has voted and will still vote like a Republican senator from Tennessee (note I'm fine with people complaining that he campaigned with Trump or that he should advocate openly for impeachment).

Wanker of the weekend: VP Pence for wasting tax dollars just so he could go to a football game for ten minutes and then leave when players kneeled for the national anthem (which he knew they would do).

(Anthony) *Weiner* of the weekend: Harvey Weinstein mostly because I just wanted to make that joke. Runner up—anyone who condemns Democrats for benefiting from the support of Weinstein while not saying the same thing about Republicans and Trump and Bill O'Reilly and Roger Ailes and…

Whopper of the weekend: "Nobody has done more for Puerto Rico than I have and gotten less credit."

Weeper of the weekend: That millions are still without power in Puerto Rico.

Wonder of the weekend: That Trump is still president of the United States of America.

OCTOBER 10, 2017: PRUITT *TRIES* TO GET *RID* OF THE CLEAN POWER PLAN

Yesterday Scott Pruitt, EPA administrator and sixth worst Trump cabinet member (may have moved into the top five with the resignation of Price), announced that he is beginning the process to repeal the signature climate change effort of the Obama administration, the Clean Power Plan.

The headlines are dramatic. "Pruitt killing the centerpiece of Obama's climate change policy" (*Newsweek*). "Trump administration to terminate Obama climate initiative" (*Chicago Tribune*).

And the stakes are big, so it makes sense for some drama here. But the headlines fail to acknowledge that this is the start of a very long process that may or may not end up with the Clean Power Plan in place. It could also end up with a stricter climate policy.

First, the Trump EPA must accept public comments for sixty days. Then they must respond to those comments. And the response can't be a simple blowoff because…

Environmental groups and states will sue over the repeal. Courts will examine everything about the repeal including the economic analysis (very scanty from what little I saw), the justification for repealing (also scanty), and how the agency responds to commenters. The court case will take a while, perhaps years after the rule is finalized some time in 2018.

This is why industry is nervous about the repeal. The effort could get overturned in court. In that case the Clean Power Plan stays in place (I'd rate this being at least 50 percent likely to happen). If the court case takes long enough or if the Trump administration does nothing to issue a new climate change policy that stands up in court (they are still legally obligated to do something), then a Democratic administration could create a new climate change regulation. And it could be stricter.

So this is an attempted repeal. And as Sideshow Bob said, "Attempted murder, what kind of crime is that? Do they give Nobel Prizes for attempted chemistry?"

OCTOBER 12, 2017: SOMEWHERE OUT THERE

Somewhere out there, there is an impressionable young voter who sees Trump's tweets attacking the press and threatening to punish them for stories he doesn't like and thinks:

- Yeah, the press is biased against my point of view.
- Yeah, even liberals admit the press protects sleazebags like Harvey Weinstein.
- Yeah, I remember that story that was wrong and that other one that was never reported.
- Yeah, the press is controlled by elitists, globalists (or some other euphemism for Jews).

Actually it's not an impressionable young voter but rather forty to sixty million voters who are having their latent authoritarian impulses being brought closer to the surface by the president. And while Trump may be too incompetent to actually follow through on his threats (assuming we don't end up in a war), the next guy five to ten years down the line might not be. He'll be able to more easily count on this base that Trump has primed. And that's why these public statements undermining our most precious freedoms are so pernicious.

OCTOBER 14, 2017: TRUMP TAKES POOR PEOPLE AND IRAN DEAL HOSTAGE

The past few days have seen Trump announce several policy initiatives that put Congress in a tough spot and the American public in a tougher one.

- He announced the ending of some Obamacare subsidies (that courts may have found unconstitutional anyway). If Congress does not restore them via statute, the individual markets could start to collapse.
- He announced he would not certify the Iran nuclear deal. This puts the future of the deal in Congress's hands (although as the article in the first comment points out Congress could do nothing and punt back to Trump).

Similarly, last month, he announced that beneficiaries of the DACA program had six months more before they needed to worry about being deported. Again, Congress could fix the problem by passing legislation protecting the dreamers.

In each of these cases, Trump, frustrated by Congress's impotence, is trying to force them to act on these policy issues. If they don't, then the welfare of those who buy health insurance on the exchanges, the future of the Iran deal, and the safety of the dreamers are severely damaged. Collectively they would be among the biggest policy impacts that Trump has had as president to date.

It's an old aphorism, "Don't take a hostage you are not prepared to shoot." In the health-care and immigration scenarios, it is clear that Trump is prepared to shoot (I'm less certain about the Iran deal) and then blame Congress for his pulling the trigger.

From a political perspective, it is pretty clear that either Trump or congressional Republicans would be hurt by the ending of these politically popular programs. But I don't think any of us want to see the hostages shot in order to get this political gain.

OCTOBER 16, 2017: NOT A GAME

Too often, particularly now in the Trump era, we look at news stories and think about how they will affect Trump or how they will affect the 2018 midterms. Trump explicitly encourages this mentality (yet another fault of his). When Trump tweets something asinine or gets into a fight with Bob Corker, having that conversation is not a bad thing.

But when he does something with significant policy implications like he did last week, taking steps that may destabilize the individual health-insurance market, it tends to lead us to lose sight of why we are fighting him.

The moves may very well hurt Trump and the Republicans politically. But in order for that to happen, lots of people have to be hurt first. They will get priced out of health-insurance markets and go back to their lives pre-Obamacare, visiting the emergency room for medical care.

Sure, some of those people voted for Trump. Some stayed home, and some voted for Hillary. But if we are to stand for anything, we can't root for people to get hurt regardless of their vote. And we can't root for them to get hurt so that the polls move.

OCTOBER 18, 2017: THE TRUMP STAIN

He's like one of those science fiction or horror creatures. Everything he touches gets poisoned, and he keeps expanding his reach. I posted a couple of weeks ago about how he has humiliated his cabinet (Sessions and Tillerson especially). On Monday, he made McConnell, whom he has attacked repeatedly, stand next to him for a press conference and stupidly smiled while he made a fool of himself.

Then there is the *New Yorker* article about Pence that makes it clear that Trump enjoys humiliating him, mocking his religious fervor, and has zero respect for him. None of these people who thought they could evade Trump's stink will get out with their reputations and dignity intact.

The problem is that he also poisons those who cross him. Jeff Flake has been a never-Trumper since the campaign. And, unless something surprising happens, his Senate career is ending some time in 2018. This is why most Republicans want to keep him at arm's length, not too close but not provoking him either.

And this is why he needs to be removed from office…before the creature destroys all of us.

OCTOBER 19, 2017: POLLING IN THE NEUTRAL ZONE

Trump's approval rating has been between thirty-seven and thirty-nine (with one brief foray above that range during Hurricanes Harvey and Irma) for five months now. That is remarkable stability for an insane period.

It has stayed there among policy disasters (the failure of the Obamacare repeal), political chaos (firings of half of his staff), idiotic tweets (NFL, Puerto Rico, so many, many more), and Charlottesville. It has also stayed there amid a booming stock market and very solid employment numbers.

I think it safe to say that at least 37 percent of the population either really likes or really wants to like Donald Trump. It is also safe to say that at least 60 percent of us think he is a raging maniac (well probably 40 percent or so and then 20 percent who have given up on him).

That's a problematic number for the GOP. It is low enough that representatives of moderate areas of the country (think Susan Collins) and those who no longer face reelection (think John McCain) can betray him safely. It is also low enough to keep the Democratic Party unified, even those from areas he carried (think Joe Manchin). But it is high enough that any Republican facing reelection has to kiss his ring or risk losing a primary (think Dean Heller).

So we are stuck here until something major moves the polls. A war (helps Trump), a stock market crash (hurts Trump), or clear evidence that Trump colluded with Russia (Lordy, I hope there are tapes) would do the trick. Until then we meander on lurching just on the right side of the border of chaos.

OCTOBER 20, 2017: POLLING IN THE NEUTRAL ZONE (PART II—THE UNANSWERABLE QUESTION)

So my post yesterday got two very different reactions (one on the thread and one in a private message). One person said that Trump's 37 percent will never leave him, and the other (a resident of a very red state) said that Republicans are already bailing in private conversations but aren't willing to admit it publicly.

This gets at the heart of a very important question. If Robert Mueller finds evidence of collusion or other crimes committed by Trump, impeachment will depend a lot on how many of those people still supporting him abandon him. If he stays in the low-mid thirties even after revelations, a Republican Congress will not move against him (although the chances of the Dems winning in 2018 go up). If his base is fraying, then his chances of staying in office decrease dramatically.

There is not a lot of evidence either way on this question. Most importantly, a survey in August showed that those who "strongly support" Trump had decreased to 24 percent. But there have been no surveys since then. Given that his approval rating has held steady, it is likely that this number hasn't moved much either.

But we won't know for sure until Trump gets much worse news than he has had so far. And Charlottesville didn't do the trick, so it's gonna have to be really bad. If we do get that really bad hit though, there is room for hope.

OCTOBER 22, 2017: SCENARIO UPDATE

Nate Silver updated his scenarios for how the Trump administration will turn out,[45] so I figure I should update mine. As a reminder, while Nate has fourteen, I only have five:

1. Slow march to impeachment
2. Sudden event prompts Trump to leave

____

45 "Where is the Trump Presidency Headed?" _Fivethirtyeight_, October 18, 2017, https://fivethirtyeight.com/features/where-is-the-trump-presidency-headed/.

3. Totalitarianism
4. Typical Republican presidency
5. Four years of chaos

I think it is time to say that #4 is very close to zero probability. There may very well be a tax cut for the wealthy and corporations, but I am willing to bet that such a tax cut will be seen as the only significant NORMAL thing about Trump's presidency when the history books are written.

As with the last time I wrote, I think scenario 3 has decreased in probability with Trump's displays of incompetence. I still think most people (including Silver) underestimate the risk but with people like Bush, Corker, and McCain speaking out, the system seems to be slowly building a firewall against the worst possible outcomes.

So that leaves, 1, 2, and 5. If I had to rank them, I would go 5, 1, and 2 but would also note that the combined probability of 1 and 2, both of which result in Trump not serving out his term, is almost equal to that of 5 and 3 combined. So if you want to sleep well, you can hang your hat on that.

OCTOBER 24, 2017: THE LOSS OF NUANCE

Last week, George W. Bush gave a speech that was a very thinly veiled criticism of Trump. It was a good speech, and Bush rightly was praised for it.

Now, however, come the think pieces. One in the *New Republic* caught my eye titled, "Liberals Stop Applauding George W. Bush." Screw that, I'm gonna applaud him.

George W. Bush was an awful president. Even if he did everything else right in his eight years in office (and he did not come close), the decisions to invade Iraq and not sign Kyoto were enough to put his balance of payments in the negative. Nothing he does or says will change the disastrous policies he put in place as president.

But that doesn't mean, we can't praise him when he does something good. And in what is a crisis of the first magnitude for the republic, being on the right side of it counts for something. We don't need to decide if he gets into The Good Place or forgive him for his presidency. We are not forever compromised if we say something nice about him.

Until Trump, every president in history did good things and did bad ones in office, before they were in office, and after they were in office. Some did many more good things (Lincoln). Some did many more bad things (Nixon). But for God's sake, I'd like to think that we can criticize the politicians we largely agree with when they do something we don't like and praise the ones we don't usually agree with when they do something we do like (still waiting for Trump on this count). If not, then we are in even more trouble than I thought (and I'm pretty worried).

OCTOBER 26, 2017: NORMS, POLITICS, AND POLICY

It has been a busy couple of days. We had the Corker and Flake denouncements of Trump, a congressional vote to protect banks from class action lawsuits, and lots of tweets (and I'm not even going into the silly stories on the Steele dossier). I want to focus a bit on the interplay of these events and refer you to the tweetstorm below as well, which makes many of these points.

1. Where Trump is doing the most damage is not in policy. He has largely been a failure in getting his agenda enacted thus far. Instead he is destroying norms, and in the process harming our standing abroad, the cause of freedom everywhere, and racial relations here, largely through his statements and tweets. He is also weakening enforcement of some laws (environment, and worker safety) while making it stronger in policing and immigration. Sadly, as long as he is in office, there is almost *nothing* that Congress and courts can do about this other than make the kinds of statements that Flake and Corker did on Tuesday. The bully pulpit and the president's power in foreign policy have few constraints.

2. The policy damage is being done in Congress. So far it has been limited, but it is not trivial. The reversal of the arbitration rule is a prime example of this. While Trump has failed in his agenda, McConnell and Ryan have gotten a few victories in theirs. These

are typically in low salience issues (ones that few pay attention to). But on higher salience issues, they are constrained by public opinion. The public reaction was a big factor in the failure of Obamacare repeal and will play a role in the outcome of the tax debate (already the plan to scrap the state or local deduction looks dead). That's why calls and protests are important. Congresspeople up for election every two years react to their public.

3. This is where Mueller comes in. Eventually he will issue a report. Before that, there will be indictments (starting with Manafort and Flynn probably). These will weaken Trump and have an effect on Congress, particularly if they affect public opinion. How much is the question? If it weakens him considerably, impeachment will become an issue. Probably not one that a Republican House will move forward on but one that will hurt their reelection prospects and help those of Democrats in 2018. If Ds take the House, then impeachment from the House is a near certainty. And the speeches by Flake and Corker (even though they will be gone by then) tell us that the Senate may take it seriously, in part because they abhor the destruction of norms and in bigger part because a Democratic House will hurt their ability to change policies.

But this process will take a while, probably through 2018. How much more will norms be weakened by Trump in that time? How bad will the tax cut that McConnell and Ryan will get be? Cloudy the future is.

OCTOBER 27, 2017: REPUBLICANS AND CONSERVATIVES

Well the free press has finally picked up on what I've been saying for months. The *Times* and *Post* both ran stories yesterday on the "split" in the Republican Party, and both (rightly in my view) concluded that the Republican Party is now Trump's party.

Corker and Flake only felt comfortable going against Trump when they no longer faced (or gave up on) reelection. They are conservatives. Conservatism has a long history (centuries, maybe millennia depending on definitions). They believe in limited government and have faith in traditional institutions like church and family. Change when it happens should happen slowly. I'm simplifying obviously.

The problem for conservatives is that their views have never held appeal to more than a slice (10, maybe 20, percent) of the American electorate. So they had to lie to that larger portion of the American electorate that either (a) liked government benefits but only for themselves or (b) didn't feel comfortable with the growing equality of women and diversity of the country. It worked for forty years—quite a run.

But these groups got tired of being used. So when Trump came along, they, vastly outnumbering the conservatives, took over the party. Now the smarter conservatives like Flake and Corker are discovering that they don't plan on giving it back.

In the next few months, we will see which conservatives have integrity and leave the GOP. The first good test is who endorses Roy Moore (very much not a conservative, very much a Trump Republican) in the December Alabama primary. Flake and Sasse yesterday said they wouldn't. Cornyn said he would as will many others who will reveal they were never conservatives but rather opportunists of the worst sort.

OCTOBER 28, 2017: FRIDAY-NIGHT INDICTS

You probably saw the news that the first charges have been filed by the grand jury convened by Mueller. More thoughts on Monday when we find out who was indicted and for what. But a couple of quick reactions.

- For Watergate buffs, this strikes me as roughly equivalent to the point where Haldeman and Ehrlichman were forced to resign. It still took sixteen months before Nixon was gone. Hopefully it is the equivalent of Haldeman and Ehrlichman being indicted, which occurred only five months before Nixon resigned.
- Trump, not as smart as Nixon as I've pointed out before, may do something to hasten the crisis. Pardon those indicted or firing Mueller are the top two possibilities.

- If that happens, we are in full blown crisis mode. It will be time to protest, call Congress daily, and so on.

OCTOBER 29, 2017: FIVE QUESTIONS FOR TOMORROW

Who will be indicted? The higher up the person (Manafort and Flynn), the worse it is for Trump.

What will they be indicted for? The closer the crime is to having something to do with collusion with Russia, the worse it is for Trump.

What does Mueller say about the indictments (if anything)? Are they the "first step in a long process" or something that feels closer to a conclusion?

How does Trump react? A tweetstorm about Hillary's collusion, noise about firing Mueller, or actually firing Mueller, pardoning whoever is indicted, a golfing trip?

How do Republican leaders react? Falling in line behind Trump or continuing to slowly distance themselves?

Buckle up, it's going to be a bumpy week.

OCTOBER 30, 2017: A GOOD DAY

Well, I spent most of the day on Twitter and did not get much work done. But at least now I can answer the five questions I asked yesterday.

Who will be indicted?

Manafort and his protégé (I want a protégé by the way—looking for volunteers) were indicted on twelve counts that could put them in jail for the rest of their lives. Meanwhile George Papadopoulos, a Trump campaign staffer, signed a plea agreement back on October 5 (but was made public today) agreeing that he lied to the FBI repeatedly about his contact with Russians. Every sign points to the release of the plea agreement on the same day as the Manafort indictments not being coincidental in timing.

What will they be indicted for?

Manafort and Gates were indicted for money laundering, tax evasion, and other crimes not explicitly related to collusion. This is not a big surprise, as prosecutors indict first where the evidence is, and apparently there is a lot of evidence for these crimes. Then you use this to try and get evidence or testimony for larger crimes. Papadopoulos pleaded to lying to the FBI (charges on other things may have been temporarily dropped pending his cooperation). While he could get five years in prison for this, his cooperation will likely result in probation. The message is clear, cooperate, and you can go free like Papadopoulos. Resist, and you can spend a long time in jail.

What does Mueller say about the indictments (if anything)? Are they the "first step in a long process" or something that feels closer to a conclusion?

Nothing. Not surprising, but wow this would be more fun if he said something. Still silence is golden from his perspective. And there is every reason to think that there is a lot more to come in this investigation.

How does Trump react? A tweetstorm about Hillary's collusion, noise about firing Mueller, or actually firing Mueller, pardoning whoever is indicted, a golfing trip?

Tweetstorm blaming Hillary. Then a secret lunch with Pence and Sessions. As despicable as those three are, I would have loved to have been a fly on the wall there.

How do Republican leaders react? Falling in line behind Trump or continuing to slowly distance themselves?

Everyone in office who has said something publicly has said that this is what Mueller was hired to do. Even spineless Paul Ryan. This is not a good sign for Trump.

A few other thoughts:

The timing of the release of Papadopoulos's plea is also likely to put pressure on Manafort and Gates as they negotiate with the prosecutor's office (I still would be surprised if Manafort flips).

Papadopoulos was arrested on July 27. If Trump wants to know how to stop leaks, he should talk to Mueller.

We know that Flynn is also guilty of at least one of the crimes Manafort was indicted for (nondisclosures). So why no indictment for Flynn? Does Mueller not have enough or is Flynn cooperating?

With Papadopoulos having talked with the Russians, while Manafort who has a history with the Russians was campaign chair for Trump, it is natural to ask what Manafort knew, and when he knew it. Then we have to ask the same thing about Trump. "What did the president know, and when did he know it?" is a question with a storied history.

In a year with very few good news days, today was a very good one.

Buckle up, it's still going to be a bumpy week.

NOVEMBER 1, 2017: TAXES AND RUSSIA

Ever since Trump took office, I've thought that the easiest policy victory for him would be a tax cut for the wealthy. Reagan got one with a Democratic Congress. We got one before 9/11 when he had middling approval ratings. Surely Trump with unified Republican control of Congress could get one. Now I'm not so sure.

Three things happened this week to give me doubts.

1. The Republicans delayed their release of the tax bill. This means they still don't have enough agreement within the party to release a bill.
2. Poll results were released showing that fewer than a third of the public support the tax plan (though no one really knows what it is yet, clearly we know enough to dislike it). This is very low considering that the opposition to the plan has not yet geared up.
3. Russia. Most importantly the Mueller revelations weaken Trump. If the tax bill is unpopular and Republicans are divided, they are going to need presidential leadership to get it passed. In addition to the fact that Trump won't even understand the bill, his eroding public support and the distraction of the Russia investigation will make it hard for him to help get it passed.

And then if the tax bill fails, Republicans in Congress will have one less reason to protect Trump from the investigation. It all fits together, and it's why we need to fight on all fronts.

NOVEMBER 2, 2017

This mailer for a school board election is from a town right next to mine in my blue state. This is what Trump wrought. If you are black, brown, Jewish, Muslim, and so on, you are in more danger from these sentiments than you were eighteen months ago. And when Trump says, "Make America Great Again," the people who sent out this flyer knew exactly what he meant.

NOVEMBER 4, 2017: THE REPUBLICAN TAX PLAN

We should think about the House GOP tax plan, unveiled Thursday, from both a policy perspective and a politics perspective. Fortunately thinking about it from a policy perspective is easy. It's awful. Like the Obamacare repeal, it is a massive reallocation of welfare up the income ladder and from blue states to red states. There are particular aspects of it that deserve more attention (the mortgage interest deduction, treatment of state and local taxes, pass through rates, etc.), frankly not all of which are awful. But none of those changes the fundamental awfulness of the bill.

The politics are more complicated. Especially since the debate will be taking place during continued Russia revelations, a need to pass a budget by December 8, the expiration of the SCHIP, and the mystery over the fate of the DACA recipients. The bill is not popular with the public, but it won't hit as many people immediately as Obamacare repeal did (and some people will be helped). The business community seems divided over it with small businesses and the real-estate industry angry, while hedge funds and multinationals are very happy (surprise!).

For the moment I will echo the caution voiced by Perry Bacon[46] "the safest thing I can say is that the tax bill has a better chance of passing than the health care bill did—but a worse chance than the Gorsuch nomination."

NOVEMBER 6, 2017: THE FIFTH AVENUE QUESTION

In January 2016, Trump said, "I could stand in the middle of Fifth Avenue and shoot somebody, and I wouldn't lose voters." It would turn out to be the most perceptive observation he has made since entering politics (I know, a low bar, but still he picked up on this when no one else did).

I suspect that we are going to test this statement in the next few months. Consider the following.

- In my view, Trump's top advisers almost certainly knew about Russian hack of the DNC e-mails and may have privately condoned it.
- In my view, the same is probably true of Trump himself.
- Trump is also likely guilty of financial crimes (like Manafort) and sexual assault.

---

46 Perry Bacon Jr., "The GOP Tax Bill Has a Chance as Long as Americans Don't Hate It," *Fivethirtyeight,* November 2, 2017, https://fivethirtyeight.com/features/the-gop-tax-bill-has-a-chance-as-long-as-americans-dont-hate-it/.

This will all come out in the months ahead. Thus far our institutions have done well in responding to Trump on thwarting his policy goals. Congress (yes, Congress), the courts, the media, and the bureaucracy have all checked him. But the test ahead is unlike anything they have faced yet.

If, when all this news comes out and Trump stays above 30 percent in the polls (I actually think 28 percent or so is the threshold, but thirty is a nice round number for the media), Republicans in Congress will have to decide, do they go after him and risk their seats or do they sit on their hands? The article below[47] points out that his voters may not be persuaded by anything Mueller finds.

Even if that is the case, I think enough congressional representatives will do something, which is why I remain cautiously optimistic. But if his voters are not persuadable, if he shoots someone and they don't care, it is possible that Trump will be found guilty of the worst stuff he's accused of and nothing will happen. That is certainly a possible outcome and should not be dismissed (my more cynical readers have voiced it). And if that occurs, then those institutions that have stood up to Trump so far will be in trouble. Our democracy will have taken a big step to neutering all institutions besides the presidency and the military. Venezuela and Turkey can tell you how that comes out.

NOVEMBER 8, 2017: A BIG DAY FOR THE DEMS

It is hard to imagine how you would write a better script for the Democrats than last night's. Phil Murphy romped to victory in my state of New Jersey. Ralph Northam won a convincing election in Virginia. Most importantly (because state legislative races are rarely if ever personality driven), the Democrats made major gains in the Virginia House of Delegates. The Medicaid expansion got approved in Maine, and the Washington state legislature flipped to the Dems. Wow. Random observations (mostly cribbed from others):

---

47 David Roberts, "America is Facing an Epistemic Crisis," *Vox.com* November 2, 2017, https://www.vox.com/policy-and-politics/2017/11/2/16588964/america-epistemic-crisis.

- Much as Obama hatred fueled Republican off year victories in 2009, 2010, and 2014, Trump hatred was the single biggest factor in the Democratic victories yesterday. Any analysis that tells you anything else is wrong. This bodes well for 2018.
- The special election results that everyone said were disappointments for Democrats were actually harbingers of last night. Dems ran better than expected in all of the congressional special elections in Republican districts and won a number of state legislative special elections over the past year in purple seats. Just as they would end up doing last night.
- Trump and Breitbart's reaction to the Gillespie loss could signal a civil war in the GOP that could make things worse for the party. Gillespie embraced Trumpism at the end of his campaign to no avail. It didn't help him beat Northam, and Trump dumped him faster than you can say bigly. The Trumpists will say that they need more genuinely racist candidates, and the establishment will try to point out that this won't work in areas outside the Deep South and the whiter sections of the plains states and Midwest. It could get ugly.
- The best thing about the Northam win is that regardless of what happens in 2018 and 2020, Virginia will not be able to gerrymander their districts because Northam will have veto powers over redistricting.
- Anyone who tells you the Democratic Party is dead is silly. Nothing helps a party more than a galvanizing figure like Trump. Just look at how Tom Perriello campaigned for Northam after losing the primary to him. This is not to say the splits in the party aren't real, they just aren't electorally important as long as Trump is in power.
- A transgender person beat the sponsor of the bathroom bill in the Virginia House of Delegates. It doesn't get any better than that.
- Two more GOP House members announced they are not running for reelection in 2018. Expect yesterday's results to prompt a few more Republicans to want to spend more time with their families.

- A year is a long time, so don't get cocky. There is a lot of work to do. But right now the chance of the Dems taking over the House in 2018 has gone above 50 percent for the first time.

NOVEMBER 9, 2017: WHY I WRITE

A year ago, it was pouring rain in New Jersey. It matched the mood in our house and at work. Trump had just been elected president, and the scenario I treated as a joke twelve months earlier, an impossibility ten months earlier, and feared but didn't think would happen a day ago had materialized. I took to Facebook. First on my personal account, and then here, I've been writing ever since.

To "celebrate" the one year anniversary, I thought it would be a good idea to go back and restate why from the first time I took Trump seriously (late February 2016), the idea of him as president terrified and appalled me. Basically, it comes down to three beliefs that have always informed my political thinking. Trump is the first person to come down on the wrong side of all three. Warning this gets long.

The first is my belief that one of the primary functions of government is to pursue fairness and justice. Much of our success depends on where we are born. If you are born white, you have a better chance of success in this country than if you are born black. If you identify as male, you will likely make more money than if you identify as female. Government can't rectify all of these unfairnesses, but it can ensure that the worst consequences of them, less access to health care, education, jobs, and a clean environment are reduced. And government should do that and strive to eliminate the conscious and unconscious discrimination that exacerbates them.

Donald Trump was born white, male, and with a fortune to his name. Being born to these categories does not ensure that you will lack recognition of the fundamental unfairnesses described above. FDR famously was a "traitor to his class" and did more to help the poor than any president before or since. But Trump not only doesn't recognize that a lack of success is often due to factors beyond people's control, he actively wants to reinforce those factors. His racist behavior goes back decades and should no longer shock anyone. He has given white supremacy the ability to feel welcome in the public square. This is reason number one that I despise him.

Reason number two is that despite the above sentiment, I also have an inherent concern about the growth of government. When governments grow powerful, they have always turned eventually to abusing that power. The power to restrict freedom and imprison people is inherent in government. Therefore, we must create government systems where accumulation of such power is limited by the rule of law and elect people who will respect those limits.

Trump is clearly not such a person. His open admiration of the most authoritarian leaders on the planet has always been there and has only been augmented by his time in office. He wants to be a dictator, and these desires have always been destined to erode our standing in the world. While it may be fashionable to be down on America, we have always stood for something to people around the world. There is a reason that despite everything so many people want to come here. That is our greatest asset, and Trump's tin-pot tendencies are quickly eroding it.

Finally, I have spent my past twenty-five years studying or working in government. Governing is a skill. It is also a calling. The people who do it, disparagingly referred to as bureaucrats, do so because they want to make the world a better place. Their bosses, disparagingly referred to as politicians, are mostly the same. They all do so knowing that their reward will be public scorn. But to do their jobs well takes years of training and practice. The jobs at the top of the hierarchy are not to be taken lightly.

Trump could not have taken them more lightly. His lack of experience has been a saving grace in some ways but a disaster in others. Departments like HUD, Education and most importantly State are led by people with no experience, and stories out of those agencies are frightening. The idea that anyone could be president, while a nice fiction, is a dangerous. Trump is not qualified for the job and that has been clear every day of the past year.

The combination of racism and entitlement, disrespect for the rule of law, and incompetence was there for everyone to see from the moment Trump descended his escalator to announce his candidacy. He's an awful man, and he's been the worst president in the country's history. And that's why I write and will keep writing until he's gone or the greatest country in the world is.

Appendix: Readings

The catastrophe that was the 2016 election has produced a ton of outstanding writing. Many of these pieces are in the largely ephemeral medium of blog posts or even vicious Twitter streams. In other words, they will soon be lost to history.

One way I coped with the shock emanating from the Trump victory is to read a great deal about the election, its causes, and its likely aftermath. One important qualification: these are pieces that I largely (perhaps not entirely) agree with. You won't see articles here about how the Democrats need to abandon identity politics or sad laments for the white working class. You also won't see analyses of the political landscape for the next few elections. Nor will you see many pieces on the likely impact of the election on specific policy issues like health care or the environment. I think that before we worry about policy areas or prospects for 2018 or 2020, we need to first guard against more fundamental threats that a Trump presidency may represent.

Here are articles that added to my understanding of our current political condition (some additional articles are referenced directly in diary entries and links to them can be found in footnotes).

THE POSSIBILITY OF FASCISM
Neal Gabler, "Farewell America," *Moyers and Company*, November 10, 2016, http://billmoyers.com/story/farewell-america/#.WDvAFLENGa.

A Twitter stream from Elliot Lusztig November 28, 2016: https://storify.com/mariahaskins/elliot-lusztig-ezlusztig-on-the-language-of-fascis.

Ned Resnikoff, "Trump's Lies Have a Purpose. They are an Assault on Democracy," *Think Progress*, November 28, 2016, https://thinkprogress.org/when-everything-is-a-lie-power-is-the-only-truth-1e641751d150#.wlnb9i3jb.

Jacob Levy, "Authoritarianism and Post-Truth Politics" *Niskanen Center*, November 30, 2016, https://niskanencenter.org/blog/authoritarianism-post-truth-politics/.

Andrea Kendall-Taylor and Erica Frantz, "How Democracies Fall Apart," *Foreign Affairs*, December 5, 2016, https://www.foreignaffairs.com/articles/2016-12-05/how-democracies-fall-apart.

Andrew Prokop, "Trump's Governing Strategy is Taking Shape and it Could be a Political Winner," *Vox.com*, December 9, 2016. http://www.vox.com/policy-and-politics/2016/12/9/13882856/trump-carrier-cabinet-puzder.

Peter Stern, "Donald Trump's Real Threat to the Press," *Politico*, December 11, 2016. http://www.politico.com/magazine/story/2016/11/donald-trumps-real-threat-to-the-press-214517.

Steven Levitsky and Daniel Ziblatt, "Is Donald Trump a Threat to Democracy," *New York Times*, December 16, 2016, http://www.nytimes.com/2016/12/16/opinion/sunday/is-donald-trump-a-threat-to-democracy.html?ref=opinion.

Sarah Kendzior, "Our Kids May Never Get the Chance to Know America," *De Correspondent*, January 19, 2017, https://thecorrespondent.com/6050/our-kids-may-never-get-the-chance-to-know-america/1711243207850-933a4d1a.

David Roberts, "Trump isn't an Evil Genius," *Vox.com* January 31, 2017, http://www.vox.com/policy-and-politics/2017/1/31/14442190/trump-is-no-evil-genius.

David Frum, "How to Build an Autocracy," *The Atlantic*, March, 2017, https://www.theatlantic.com/magazine/archive/2017/03/how-to-build-an-autocracy/513872/.

Andres Miguel Rondon, "Donald Trump's Fictional America," *Politico* April 2, 2017, http://www.politico.com/magazine/story/2017/04/donald-trumps-fictional-america-post-fact-venezuela-214973.

Bernard Weisberger, "Red Alert: The First Amendment is in Danger," *Moyers and Company*, June 2, 2017, http://billmoyers.com/story/red-alert-first-amendment-danger/.

Masha Gessen, "Trump's Hoodlums" *New York Review of Books*, August 28, 2017, http://www.nybooks.com/daily/2017/08/29/trumps-hoodlums/.

HOW TO RESPOND IF THAT POSSIBILITY BECOMES REAL

Masha Gessen, "Autocracy: Rules for Survival," *New York Review of Books*, November 10, 2016, http://www.nybooks.com/daily/2016/11/10/trump-election-autocracy-rules-for-survival/

Liel Leibovitz, "What to do About Trump? The Same Thing my Grandfather Did in 1930s Vienna," *Tablet*, November 14, 2016 http://www.tabletmag.com/jewish-news-and-politics/217831/what-to-do-about-trump.

Masha Gessen, "Trump, The Choice We Face," *New York Review of Books*, November 27, 2016, http://www.nybooks.com/daily/2016/11/27/trump-realism-vs-moral-politics-choice-we-face/.

Masha Gessen, "Lessons from Russia: Verify Everything, Don't Publish Rumors," *New York Times*, January 14, 2017, https://www.nytimes.com/2017/01/14/opinion/sunday/lessons-from-russia-verify-everything-dont-publish-rumors.html?_r=0.

Beverly Gage, "Reading the Classic Novel that Predicted Trump," *New York Times* January 17, 2017, https://www.nytimes.com/2017/01/17/books/review/classic-novel-that-predicted-trump-sinclar-lewis-it-cant-happen-here.html?_r=0.

Dylan Matthews, "Donald Trump, the Refugee Ban and The Triumph of Cruelty," *Vox.com*, January 28, 2017, http://www.vox.com/2017/1/28/14425354/donald-trump-cruelty.

Ezra Klein, "How to Stop an Autocracy," *Vox.com*, February 7, 2017, http://www.vox.com/policy-and-politics/2017/2/7/14454370/trump-autocracy-congress-frum.

Congressman Adam Schiff, "The Rise of the Autocrats," *Lawfare*, March 22, 2017, https://lawfareblog.com/rise-autocrats.

David Leonhardt, "The Urgency of Ethnic Nationalism," *New York Times*, April 25, 2017, https://www.nytimes.com/2017/04/25/opinion/le-pen-trump-ethnic-nationalism.html?ref=opinion.

THE ELECTION ITSELF

Andrew Flowers, "Where Trump Got His Edge," *FiveThirtyEight*, November 11, 2016, http://fivethirtyeight.com/features/where-trump-got-his-edge/.

Kelly Kleiman, "Don't Just Do Something, Stand There," *The Reality Based Community*, November 12, 2016, http://www.samefacts.com/2016/11/elections/2016/dont-just-do-something-stand-there-2/.

Harry Enten, "Demographics Isn't Destiny and Four Other Things this Election Taught Me," *FiveThirtyEight*, November 14, 2016, http://fivethirtyeight.com/features/demographics-arent-destiny-and-four-other-things-this-election-taught-me/.

David Roberts, "Everything Mattered: Lessons from 2016's Bizarre Presidential Election," *Vox.com*, November 30, 2016, http://www.vox.com/policy-and-politics/2016/11/30/13631532/everything-mattered-2016-presidential-election.

Harry Enten, "It's Not All About Clinton, The Midwest was Getting Redder Before 2016," *FiveThirtyEight*, December 9, 2016, http://fivethirtyeight.com/features/its-not-all-about-clinton-the-midwest-was-getting-redder-before-2016/.

Kevin Drum, "Stop It! There are no Big Lessons from the 2016 Election," *Mother Jones*, December 14, 2016, http://www.motherjones.com/kevin-drum/2016/12/stop-it-there-are-no-big-lessons-2016-election.

Kevin Drum, "In Iowa, It's All About Terrorists and Welfare Bums," *Mother Jones*, January 12, 2017, http://www.motherjones.com/kevin-drum/2017/01/iowa-its-all-about-terrorists-and-welfare-bums.

Nate Silver, "The Real Story of 2016," *FiveThirtyEight*, January 17. 2017, https://fivethirtyeight.com/features/the-real-story-of-2016/.

Michael Kruse, "What Do You Do if a Red State Moves to You?" *Politico*, January/February 2017, http://www.politico.com/magazine/story/2017/01/blue-red-state-democrats-trump-country-214647.

Sean McElwee and Jason McDaniel, "Fear of Diversity Made People More Likely to Vote for Trump," *The Nation*, March 14, 2017, https://www.thenation.com/article/fear-of-diversity-made-people-more-likely-to-vote-trump/.

A Twitter Storm from T. R. Ramachandran, April 1, 2017, http://electionado.com/canvas/1491097261943.

Ezra Klein, "Here's the Real Reason Hillary Clinton Lost the Election," *CNBC*, June 2, 2017, https://www.cnbc.com/2017/06/02/why-im-defending-hillary-clinton-commentary.html.

Ezra Klein "Why Did the 2016 Election Look so Much Like the 2012 Election," *Vox.com*, June 5, 2017, https://www.vox.com/policy-and-politics/2017/6/5/15161442/2016-election-normalcy-democracy-real-ists-identity.

DEMOCRATIC STRATEGY MOVING FORWARD

Jamelle Bouie, "Keep Hope Alive," *Slate*, November 27, 2016, http://www.slate.com/articles/news_and_politics/cover_story/2016/11/jesse_jackson_s_presidential_campaigns_offer_a_road_map_for_democrats_in.html.

Bill Fletcher Jr. and Bob Wing, "Fighting Back Against the White Revolt" *Verso*, December 1, 2016, http://www.versobooks.com/blogs/2986-fighting-back-against-the-white-revolt.

Will Caskey, "I Haven't Learned Anything and Don't Know What to do." *Medium* January 25, 2017, https://medium.com/@willcaskey/i-havent-learned-anything-and-don-t-know-what-to-do-c84889762eac#.avlx1p4ii.

A Twitter storm from Josh Chafetz, February 5, 2017, https://twitter.com/joshchafetz/status/828323307370778624.

Zach Beauchamp, "No Easy Answers, Why Left-Wing Economics is Not the Answer to Right-Wing Populism," *Vox.com*, March 13, 2017, http://www.vox.com/world/2017/3/13/14698812/bernie-trump-corbyn-left-wing-populism.

THE ALT-RIGHT AND THE ROLE OF RACISM

Mike Pesca, "The Alt-Right is Using Trump," *Slate*, November 23, 2016, http://www.slate.com/articles/news_and_politics/gist/2016/11/ben_shapiro_on_steve_bannon_the_alt_right_and_why_the_left_needs_to_turn.html.

Colin Taylor, "It's Like Christmas, America's Neo-Nazis Celebrate Trump's Cabinet Picks," *OccupyDemocrats*, November 18, 2016, http://

occupydemocrats.com/2016/11/18/like-christmas-americas-neo-nazis-celebrate-trumps-cabinet-picks/.

Jonathan Chait, "Donald Trump is Building a Team of Racists," *New York*, November 18, 2016, http://nymag.com/daily/intelligencer/2016/11/donald-trump-building-team-of-racists.html.

Jenee Desmond Harris, "A Pollster on the Racial Panic Obama's Presidency Triggered, and What Democrats Must Do Now," *Vox.com*, December 12, 2016, http://www.vox.com/identities/2016/12/12/13894546/obama-race-black-white-house-cornell-belcher-racism.

Jacob Levy, "The Defense of Liberty Can't Do Without Identity Politics," *Niskanen Center* December 13, 2016, https://niskanencenter.org/blog/defense-liberty-cant-without-identity-politics/.

Michael Eric Dyson, "What Donald Trump Doesn't Know About Black People," *New York Times*, December 17, 2016, http://www.nytimes.com/2016/12/17/opinion/sunday/what-donald-trump-doesnt-know-about-black-people.html.

W. David Ball, "Attention White People: Your Economic Grievances Do Not Excuse Your Racism," *The Reality Based Community*, November 10, 2016, http://www.samefacts.com/2016/11/race-and-racism/attention-white-people-your-economic-grievances-do-not-excuse-your-racism/.

Susan McWilliams, "This Political Theorist Predicted the Rise of Trump: His Name was Hunter S. Thompson," *Nation*, December 15, 2016, https://www.thenation.com/article/this-political-theorist-predicted-the-rise-of-trumpism-his-name-was-hunter-s-thompson/.

John Blake, "How Trump's Victory Turns into Another 'Lost Cause'" *CNN* December 28, 2016, http://www.cnn.com/2016/12/28/us/lost-cause-trump/index.html.

Chauncey DeVega, "It Was the Racism Stupid, White Working Class 'Economic Anxiety' is a Zombie Idea that Needs to Die,' *Salon*, January 5, 2017, http://www.salon.com/2017/01/05/it-was-the-racism-stupid-white-working-class-economic-anxiety-is-a-zombie-idea-that-needs-to-die/.

Rick Perlstein, "Peter's Choice," *Mother Jones*, January/February 2017, http://www.motherjones.com/politics/2017/01/donald-trump-2016-election-oklahoma-working-class/.

A Twitter storm from Elliott Lusztig, February 6, 2017. https://twitter.com/ezlusztig/status/828562689953767424.

Jamelle Bouie, "Government by White Nationalism is Upon Us," *Slate* February 6, 2017. http://www.slate.com/articles/news_and_politics/cover_story/2017/02/government_by_white_nationalism_is_upon_us.html?wpsrc=sh_all_dt_tw_ru.

Sarah Jones, "Trump Has Turned the GOP Into the Party of Eugenics," *New Republic*, February 15, 2017, https://newrepublic.com/article/140641/trump-turned-gop-party-eugenics.

A Twitter storm from Eric Garland, March 1, 2017, https://twitter.com/ericgarland/status/837075112075522049.

Rick Perlstein, "I Thought I Understood the American Right, Trump Proved me Wrong," *New York Times*, April 11, 2017, https://mobile.nytimes.com/2017/04/11/magazine/i-thought-i-understood-the-american-right-trump-proved-me-wrong.html.

Emma Green, "Why the Charlottesville Marchers Were Obsessed With Jews," *The Atlantic*, August 15, 2017, https://www.theatlantic.com/politics/archive/2017/08/nazis-racism-charlottesville/536928/.

Josh Marshall, "The House is on Fire – Accepting the Truth of the Trump Revolution," *TPM*, August 16, 2017, http://talkingpoints-memo.com/edblog/the-house-is-on-fire-accepting-the-truth-of-the-trump-revolution.

Josh Marshall "Some Thoughts on Public Memory," *TPM*, August 14, 2017, http://talkingpointsmemo.com/edblog/some-thoughts-on-public-memory.

THE DECLINE OF INSTITUTIONS

Fareed Zakaria, "America's Democracy Has Become Illiberal," *Washington Post*, December 29, 2016, https://www.washingtonpost.com/opinions/america-is-becoming-a-land-of-less-liberty/2016/12/29/2a91744c-ce09-11e6-a747-d03044780a02_story.html?tid=sm_fb&utm_term=.3860969f9474.

Jacob Levy, "The Party Declines," *Niskanen Center*, January 18, 2017, https://niskanencenter.org/blog/the-party-declines/.

Jon Rauch, "How American Politics Went Insane," *The Atlantic* July/August 2017 http://www.theatlantic.com/magazine/archive/2016/07/how-american-politics-went-insane/485570/.

RUSSIA AND GLOBAL THREATS TO DEMOCRACY

A Twitter storm from Eric Garland, December 11, 2016 https://twitter.com/ericgarland/status/808045818024497157.

A Twitter storm from Eric Garland, January 2, 2017, https://twitter.com/ericgarland/status/816099810696720384.

Anne Applebaum, "An Existential Moment for the Euro-American Alliance," *Washington Post*, January 5, 2017https://www.washington-post.com/opinions/global-opinions/an-existential-moment-for-the-euro-american-alliance/2017/01/05/23407646-d360-11e6-945a-76f69a399dd5_story.html.

David Remnick, "Trump, Putin, and the Big Hack," *The New Yorker,* January 6, 2017, http://www.newyorker.com/news/news-desk/trump-putin-and-the-big-hack.

Kenneth Roth, "The Dangerous Rise of Populism" *Human Rights Watch,* January 2017, https://www.hrw.org/world-report/2017/country-chapters/dangerous-rise-of-populism.

Robert Kagan, "The Twilight of the Liberal World Order," *Brookings,* January 24, 2017, https://www.brookings.edu/research/the-twilight-of-the-liberal-world-order/.

A Twitter storm from Seth Abrahamson, March 13, 2017, https://twitter.com/SethAbramson/status/841352797559881729.

A Twitter storm from Seth Abrahamson, May 23, 2017, https://twitter.com/sethabramson/status/867172280350146561.

POSTINAUGURATION

Elliot Cohen, "A Clarifying Moment in American History" *The Atlantic,* January 29, 2017, https://www.theatlantic.com/politics/archive/2017/01/a-clarifying-moment-in-american-history/514868/.

Nate Silver, "14 Versions of Trump's Presidency, From MAGA to Impeachment," *FiveThirtyEight,* February 3, 2017, https://fivethirtyeight.com/features/14-versions-of-trumps-presidency-from-maga-to-impeachment/.

Fintan O'Toole, "Welcome to Trumperica," *The Irish Times,* February 4, 2017, http://www.irishtimes.com/news/world/us/fintan-o-toole-welcome-to-trumperica-1.2960823#.WJXOYJZdBNA.twitter.

David Rothkopf, "The Shallow State," *Foreign Policy*, February 22, 2017, http://foreignpolicy.com/2017/02/22/the-shallow-state-trump/.

Sarah Kendzior, "Want to Survive Another 100 Days of Trump? Don't Get Complacent," *The Globe and Mail*, May 1, 2017, https://beta.theglobeandmail.com/opinion/trump-100-days-survive-dont-get-complacent/article34853406/?ref=http://www.theglobeandmail.com&service=mobile.

A Twitter Storm from Eric Garland, May 28, 2017, https://twitter.com/ericgarland/status/868940201426595841.

Josh Marshall, "The Madness of King Trump," *TPM*, June 5, 2017, http://talkingpointsmemo.com/edblog/the-madness-of-king-trump.

Michael Lewis, "Why the Scariest Nuclear Threat may be Coming From Inside the White House," *Vanity Fair*, July 26, 2017, http://www.vanityfair.com/news/2017/07/department-of-energy-risks-michael-lewis.

THE TRUMP FBI INVESTIGATION AND IMPEACHMENT AS A POSSIBILITY

Walter Shapiro, "James Comey and the Art of the Shiv," *Roll Call*, March 21, 2017, http://admin.rollcall.com/news/opinion/james-comey-donald-trump-russia#undefined.uxfs.

Zack Beauchamp, "The FBI Probe into Trump and Russia is Huge News. Our Political System Isn't Ready for It," *Vox.com*, March 21, 2017, http://www.vox.com/world/2017/3/21/14983550/fbi-russia-trump-hearing-partisanship.

David Hopkins, "Why Congressional Republicans Won't Abandon Trump over Comey," *Honest Graft*, May 11, 2017, http://www.honestgraft.com/2017/05/why-congressional-republicans-wont.html.

Julia Azari, "Presidential Impeachments are About Politics, Not Law," *Vox.com*, May 15. 2017, https://www.vox.com/mischiefs-of-faction/ 2017/5/15/15638286/presidential-impeachments-political.

Benjamin Wittes, "On the 'Nature of the Person:' Initial Thoughts on James Comey's Testimony," *Lawfare*, June 8, 2017, https://lawfareblog. com/nature-person-initial-thoughts-james-comeys-testimony.

Elizabeth Drew, "Trump: The Presidency in Peril," *New York Review of Books*, June 22, 2017, http://www.nybooks.com/articles/2017/06/22/ trump-presidency-in-peril/.

Josh Marshall, "The Big Trumpers Still Don't Get the Trouble they are in," *TPM*, July 12, 2017, http://talkingpointsmemo.com/edblog/ the-big-trumpers-still-dont-get-the-trouble-theyre-in.

Andrew McCarthy, "Trump, Russia and the Misconduct of Public Men," *National Review*, July 12, 2017, http://www.nationalreview.com/ article/449401/trump-jr-emails-high-crimes-misdemeanors.

Nate Silver, "Trump and Russia are Probably on a Collision Course over Russia," *FiveThirtyEight*, July 26, 2017, https://fivethirtyeight.com/fea- tures/trump-and-congress-are-probably-on-a-collision-course-over- russia/.

Jane Chong and Benjamin Wittes, "It's Time: Congress Needs to Open a Formal Impeachment Inquiry," *Lawfare*, August 28, 2017, https://lawfareblog.com/its-time-congress-needs-open-formal- impeachment-inquiry.

Bob Bauer, "A President's Words Matter, Part II: Impeachment Standards and the Case of the Demagogue," *Lawfare*, October 11, 2017, https://www.lawfareblog.com/presidents-words-matter-part-ii- impeachment-standards-and-case-demagogue.

Matthew Kahn, "How Unraveled Does Trump Have to Be? Presidential Disability and the 25th Amendment," *Lawfare*, October 23, 2017, https://www.lawfareblog.com/how-unraveled-does-trump-have-be-presidential-disability-and-25th-amendment.

GENERAL

Stephen Greenblatt, "Shakespeare Explains the 2016 Election," *New York Times* October 8, 2016, http://www.nytimes.com/2016/10/09/opinion/sunday/shakespeare-explains-the-2016-election.html?_r=0.

Benjamin Hart, "I Talked to some Trump Voters Too," *The Awl*, November 2, 2016, https://theawl.com/i-talked-to-some-trump-voters-too-24d8399a6147#.1pvfd0qjk

Chemi Shaley, "The Unbearable Stupidity of Donald Trump's Election," *Haaretz*, November 28, 2016, http://www.haaretz.com/world-news/u-s-election-2016/1.755553.

Ian Buruma, "The End of the Anglo-American Order," *New York Times*, November 29, 2016, http://www.nytimes.com/2016/11/29/magazine/the-end-of-the-anglo-american-order.html?_r=0.

David Remnick, "Obama Reckons with a Trump Presidency," *The New Yorker*, November 28, 2016, http://www.newyorker.com/magazine/2016/11/28/obama-reckons-with-a-trump-presidency.

David Greenberg, "An Intellectual History of Trumpism," *Politico*, December 11, 2016, http://www.politico.com/magazine/story/2016/12/trumpism-intellectual-history-populism-paleoconservatives-214518.

Daniel Drezner, "Donald Trump's Three Types of Norm Violations," *Washington Post*, December 19, 2016, https://www.washingtonpost.com/posteverything/wp/2016/12/19/donald-trumps-three-types-of-norm-violations/.

Eric Garland, "Why Conventional Wisdom is Dangerous and Crazy Scenarios Aren't" December 30, 2016, http://www.ericgarland.co/2016/12/30/conventional-wisdom-crazy-scenarios/.

Alan Draper, "How Dwindling Union Power Helped Usher in Trump," *The American Prospect*, January 2, 2017, http://prospect.org/article/how-dwindling-union-power-helped-usher-trump.

Masha Gessen, "In Praise of Hypocrisy,' *New York Times*, February 18, 2017, https://www.nytimes.com/2017/02/18/opinion/sunday/in-praise-of-hypocrisy.html?_r=0.

Jim Wright, "The Hubris of Ignorance," *Stonekettle Station*, April 19, 2017, http://www.stonekettle.com/2017/04/the-hubris-of-ignorance.html?spref=fb.

Adam Serwer, "The Lesser Part of Valor," *The Atlantic*, May 26, 2017, https://www.theatlantic.com/politics/archive/2017/05/the-better-part-of-valor/528384/.